Designing and Implementing an Integrated Curriculum

ISBN 0-9627232-7-4

Designing and Implementing an Integrated Curriculum

A Student-Centered Approach

Edward T. Clark, Jr.

Holistic Education Press
Brandon, VT 05733-0328
1-800-639-4122
http://www.sover.net/~holistic
holistic@sover.net

This book is dedicated
to the memory of our son, Tom,
and my brother, Jim.

They would have flourished
in the kind of school I describe.

Designing and Implementing an Integrated Curriculum

Foreword

"Will we have any more wars?" "Is there going to be enough room for landfills?" "Why am I here?" "Does the ozone layer get thinner every day?" "When will racism end?" "Will there be another depression?" "Why can't we help all of the suffering people?"

These are not topics from a PBS documentary series. No, they are actual questions that students in grades 6, 7, and 8 are asking. How do I know? I've sat in many classrooms and listened as teachers asked students what they cared about and what they wanted to learn. I would like to think that the students and staff at Thompson Middle School have *always* investigated these type of questions, but I know better. It took our first workshop with Dr. Ed Clark to start the process — and nothing has been the same since then.

It all started rather innocently with a week-long workshop titled "Integrating the Curriculum." As a staff, we had been involved with many changes in the late 80s and early 90s, and the buzz of "integration" was getting louder. By that time we had dismantled our tracking system and were knee deep in implementing cooperative learning strategies. Still, we were not satisfied. Something was missing and we thought that maybe it was the curriculum. Enter Ed Clark.

It is difficult to convey the full flavor of the systemic change that has taken place at Thompson Middle School. Since that first intensive experience in the summer of 1992 we have learned and are continuing to learn so very much. The experience of hearing students' real questions has been one of the most startling revelations that we have had. We had always thought we were meeting the needs of our customers, that we were student-centered, but their questions were nothing like the curriculum that we had been delivering through textbooks. Now with Ed's guidance, this goal is actually being realized. Customer focus means student-centered, and student-centered means, "Ask them!" Since we began to discover what students were really thinking and asking, it would be impossible to go back and organize our curriculum around those textbooks that are largely irrelevant to the lives of our students.

Perhaps the most important lesson that we have learned at Thompson is that in order to implement a new theory, one must acquire a new mindset. Just as a blueprint provides a shape for the way a builder must think, so a theory provides a shape for the mindset teachers need if they are to design an integrated curriculum. When the builder is in synch with the blueprint, he will find ways to implement the vision in spite of the many barriers he might encounter.

So it was when we began to design our new curriculum. The vision that grew from Dr. Clark's workshops is entering its fourth year of development at TMS. As we have confronted the issues of student-centered learning, we have found ourselves struggling to identify our own core values — the real reasons that we entered the teaching profession. We have recognized that this is the type of education that each one of us truly believed in but never had the opportunity to deliver. Now, as we transform our teaching from content-driven to student-initiated, we are finding that we are sustained by our own internal value structures. The frustration and excitement of our work is that we are both discovering and creating the future at the same time! Because we truly believe that what we are doing is best for our students, we are finding ways to remove the barriers which stand between us and actualizing our vision. At Thompson, because of the mutual support derived from the energy, excitement, and tenacity of the staff, the hard work of eliminating barriers goes on day after day. It seems that we are involved in a domino effect: Once the first barrier fell, the next one was a little easier to remove, and then the next, and the next....

The most significant experience that we have had during this process of eliminating barriers is our participation in the coaching sessions which Ed and I have conducted with our interdisciplinary teaching teams. Each team consists of teachers who represent language arts, math, reading, social studies, and science. The teams set their own agenda and their two half-day sessions each semester are usually a combination of assessment and planning. Here we experience the push and pull of professionals struggling in ways that model the process being followed in their classrooms. We learned quite early that the conversations that take place in a multi disciplinary team are quite different from those that occur when teachers are talking with their counterparts in science, math, or literature. In the team coaching sessions we are *all* students, asking each other tough questions like "Why do we need to know that?" or "Do you really need to spend all of that time on dividing fractions?" or "What is it you really want the kids to be able to do?" It is now the culture of Thompson Middle School that teachers frequently get together to talk formally and informally about teaching and learning. This is the direct result of Ed's coaching sessions and has become the hallmark of our professional growth. These sessions have become the lifeblood of our school.

The book you now hold in your hands contains the essence of the workshops that Dr. Clark has conducted here and elsewhere across the country. His perspective has stimulated and sustained us as we have reconstructed our curriculum. May it be as effective for you!

— Kurt Anderson, Principal
Thompson Middle School
St. Charles, Illinois

Introduction

Do not blame teachers or their administrators if they fail to educate, to change their students. For the task of *preventing* the new generation from changing in any deep or significant way is precisely what most societies require of their educators. (George Leonard)

A certain naivete is prerequisite to all learning. A certain optimism is prerequisite to all action. When a nation's best minds desert all hope and decry all enthusiasm, they leave the nation susceptible to nihilism and anarchy. When they refuse to be committed, they leave commitment to those who would destroy, not build, those who would go back, not forward. Existential despair is the ultimate copout. (G. Leonard)

Every transformation ... has rested on a new metaphysical and ideological base; or rather, upon deeper stirrings and intuitions whose rationalized expression takes the form of a new picture of the cosmos and the nature of man. (Lewis Mumford)

On occasion someone asks me whether I am optimistic or pessimistic about the future. I always tell them that I am an unreconstructed optimist, although I do admit that at times my optimism is only at a 51% level.

Perhaps educators are more optimistic than other people. They are, after all, preparing the next generation to run the country if not the world. Their focus should be, to some extent at least, on the future. Whenever I hear teachers bemoan the fact that certain students aren't living up to their potential, I am reminded that many teachers really are visionaries. They can see potential that is often hidden from others.

This is as it should be because in committing the future of our children into the hands of teachers, we are committing the future of our entire society — and perhaps humankind — into their hands. But there is a great irony here. In the past teachers have been the "keepers of tradition" whose responsibility was to *prevent* the new generation from changing in any deep or significant way. Today, their role is radically different. In a society that is changing as rapidly and dramatically as ours, teachers have become, whether they like it or not, change agents. Unlike a keeper of tradition, the change agent's responsibility is to prepare the new generation for a journey to a destination for which even the most enlightened adults are Ill-prepared.

Far more than the average parent today, teachers will, of necessity, prepare our youth and guide them on their journey into the future. In the process they will either empower or disempower our children. They will teach them to ask questions or children will learn to wait passively for someone else's answer. They will teach the next generation to evaluate themselves according to their own standards of excellence, or their students will learn to let others evaluate them by someone else's standards. They will teach kids to think for themselves or the kids will learn to allow others to do the thinking for them. They will teach them that each one has unique capacities which are worthy of nurture, or our children will learn that it is much better to suppress uniqueness so as to conform to some societal norm. In short, today's teachers are the ones who will shape the ideas and the behavior of students who, in turn, will shape the future — of our country, of Western civilization, of the Earth.

This is an awesome responsibility. Most teachers take their work seriously. While at some subliminal level many are aware of how important their work is, my experience suggests that few have raised this awareness to a conscious level. After all, they, too, are part of a culture that, in spite of its rhetoric, values conformity and, except within a narrow range of possibilities, discourages innovative ideas, creative thinking, and imaginative visions.

Given this context, this book has a three-fold purposes. First, I hope that it will raise the level of awareness among educators concerning the vital function that they play in anticipating and preparing our youth for the future. Second, I hope it will awaken readers to the tremendous potential that lies dormant in our youth. And finally, I hope it will provide a useful vision and blueprint for designing a curriculum which will tap and unleash this tremendous potential.

Readers who are looking for a step-by-step curriculum outline may be disappointed. However, although this book does emphasize the theoretical basis of an integrated, student-centered curriculum, it also provides examples of curriculum designs developed by several schools. It also addresses the process of implementing the new curricula. Finally, this book suggests practical guidelines that any teacher — regardless of grade level or student ability — can use to design an integrated curriculum.

This is the third draft edition of a book that has been more than ten years in the making. What makes this book different from earlier drafts is the experiential and anecdotal evidence of what works and what doesn't work provided by the teachers and students at Thompson Middle School in St. Charles, Illinois. Although I have been associated with teacher education for thirty years, I have learned many new lessons these past three years working with principal Kurt Anderson and the teachers and students at Thompson. Perhaps the most fundamental of these is that change is not easy or quick in coming. Regardless of how enthusiastically a teacher may embrace a new vision and blueprint for change, it takes time, energy, and a great deal of determination, encouragement, and support to risk radical change. Another lesson has been the realization that once teachers begin to internalize new ideas, their commitment and determination is inspiring and contagious. During these three years I have also learned the meaning and importance of patient, dedicated, supportive leadership. I have witnessed at Thompson a leadership style that points the direction, honors diversity and individual choice, encourages risk-taking and, then, to use Kurt's words, "gets out of the way." The result is that Thompson has become an exciting and enriching learning community. Though far from ideal, Thompson is a model of what schools can become. I only wish my own children could have been students in a school like this.

And so, I want to give a special thanks to Kurt and the faculty at Thompson — especially those whose comments, evaluations, and anecdotes enrich these pages. Among these I include Bill O'Hagan, Sharon Mulcahy, Jean Humke, Bonnie Pettebone, Sharon Young, Barb Gudvangen, Peg Anderson, Chuck Robinson, Mary Pat Ryan, Lin Stacy, Doug Lakin, Doug Thompson, Joanna Martin, Janet Fosnot, Chris Sherman, Jan Sutfin, Donna Stockman, Bob Brill, Dan Kroll, and Rex Troyer. In addition, I want to express appreciation to Judy Bock, Claudette Rasmussen, and Jean Smith who gave a full weekend of their time to help design the first complete Contextual Matrix around the question, "What does it mean to be human?"

I also want to thank my wife of 45 years, Margaret. Her persistence and support kept me "on task" and provided the wide variety of feedback — some welcome, and some not so welcome — which is so necessary in a project such as this. Appreciation also goes to graphic designer Chris Whildin, a friend and sometimes colleague, who did the final design work on the figures in this book.

And finally, my thanks goes to Charles Jakiela, my friend, my editor and my publisher. He has listened closely and thoughtfully, been astute and penetrating in his critique, and supportive throughout. Had I not trusted his insights, experience, and integrity as I do, this book would never have been completed.

I also want to note that much of the material described herein has been incorporated into an educational program called *Ecoliteracy*, which was created by Fritjof Capra, Carole Cooper, and myself. *Ecoliteracy* has many facets, all of which reflect the fundamental principles and properties of ecological systems. The program's flexibility and universal application is reflected in the fact that Fritjof, Carole, and I have each focused our work in different arenas related to educational transformation. I wish to express my appreciation to Fritjof and Carole for their contributions to both my personal and professional odysseys.

The completion of this book, like the completion of an essay or article, creates a problem for me: the day after the manuscript has been accepted, I will think of some revision that I would dearly love to make. And, I am sure that those who read and interact thoughtfully with what I have written will have ideas for their own revisions. That's as it should be because education is, at its best, a dialogue in which each participant becomes both teacher and learner. And so I welcome your participation in an on-going conversation — a kind of systemic feedback process — which encourages the questions and responses triggered by the ideas and strategies presented here. While I may not be able to interact with you directly, I promise to give thoughtful reflection to each response. Please send your feedback to me c/o Holistic Education Press, P. O. Box 328, Brandon, VT.

— Ed Clark

Chapter One

Educational Reform: A Design Problem

> If an unfriendly foreign power had attempted to impose on Americans the mediocre educational performance that exists today, we might well have viewed it as an act of war.

> Educational reform should focus on the goal of creating a Learning Society.... The goal must be to develop the talents of all to their fullest.... At the heart of such a society is the commitment to a set of values and to a system of education that affords all members the opportunity to stretch their minds to full capacity, from early childhood through adulthood, learning more as the world itself changes. Such a society has as a basic foundation the idea that education is important not only because of what it contributes to one's career goals but also because of the value it adds to the general quality of one's life. (*A Nation at Risk* 1983)

It is no secret that public education simply is not working in this country. In fact, if statistics are a valid indicator (as many as one-fourth of those who graduate from high school are not functionally literate), it hasn't been working for some time. It certainly isn't for lack of trying. Ever since the publication of *A Nation At Risk* in 1983, education has received a great deal of attention. However, in spite of many new and innovative programs such as Cooperative Learning, Whole Language and Outcome Based Education, in the words of Charles McDowell of PBS's *Washington Week in Review* each year on the anniversary of *A Nation at Risk*, "Nothing much has changed."

In 1993, the Education Commission of the States reported that fewer than 1% of the nation's schools have completed the process of restructuring, while less than 5% of the remainder had embarked on the process. At that time, fully 95% of America's schools seemed locked in the status quo (Smith 1995). As we reach the end of the millennium, schools are little different from those observed by journalist Charles Silberman's (1970) more than a quarter of a century ago.

> The public schools are the kind of institution one cannot really dislike until one gets to know them well. Because the adults take the schools so much for granted, they fail to appreciate what grim, joyless places most American schools are, how oppressive and petty are the rules by which they are governed, how intellectually sterile and aesthetically barren the atmosphere, what an appalling lack of civility obtains on the part of teachers and principals, what contempt they unconsciously display for children as children.

This has occurred not because of a lack of commitment on the part of teachers, most of whom are among the hardest working, most responsible, and lowest paid of professional workers in our society. Most are dedicated far beyond the call of duty. Why else would anyone deliberately choose a vocation which required that they supervise, monitor, and teach 25 to 30 restless children for six hours a day — kids who would often rather be anywhere else than in school! I have long believed that teachers have had a bum rap in our society.

If it's not for lack of innovative programs and it's not teachers, what is the problem? Businessman and corporate consultant Paul Hawken (1993) suggests that whenever we have systems that aren't achieving the ends we seek, we have a design problem. This means that the problems and dilemmas are the result of the way the system is designed and no amount of tinkering or "problem-solving" can correct the problem. Hierarchial systems, e.g., governments, corporations, schools, and the military, were designed to maintain the status quo. There is no way that these systems *as they are presently structured* can adapt to the rapid transitions and emerging crises that confront us. While these systems have served us well in the past, as Hawken points out, the only way to make them serve today's requirements is to change their fundamental design. Unfortunately, as Alfie Kohn (1986) observes, there is an "entrenched reluctance of Americans to consider structural explanations for problems.... We prefer to hold individuals responsible for whatever happens." In our aversion to acknowledging the existence of structural problems we are like "the cartoon animals on Sunday morning TV who continue to run even when there is no longer any ground under their feet — at least until they look down. It is as if some combination of ignorance and momentum allows them to keep going."

In short, in typical problem-solving fashion, our approach to educational reform has been to apply Band-Aids to the obvious symptoms while ignoring the more serious life-threatening condition. This is why the many exciting, innovative programs have had little substantive impact on what happens in our schools. Each of these programs reflects an attempt to treat a symptom, that is, to fix a particular piece of the problem. For example, Cooperative Learning seeks to transform the way classrooms are organized for teaching and learning by encouraging peer learning. Whole Language programs provide teachers with new insights as to how reading and writing are actually learned and experienced, while Outcome Based Education challenges teachers to pay more attention to the desired outcomes of educational practices. The difficulty is that teachers are attempting to cure one aspect of an unhealthy system and, because of the system's faulty structure, the program doesn't work and soon is abandoned. As a consequence, teachers have become tired and skeptical of any reform program because, even when they are taken seriously, they don't make that much difference in the long run.

The Real Problem

This problem-solving strategy — attempting to cure the illness by treating the symptoms — is implicit in *A Nation at Risk* and is reflected in virtually every major report that has followed. Embedded in each report is the tacit assumption that substantive educational reform would follow once we changed the prescribed goals of education. For example, *A Nation at Risk* identified what was essentially a new and certainly appropriate mission for education — "learning how to learn" and a "commitment to lifelong learning." But the report's recommendations seemed to assume that the way to achieve this new mission was by more efficient application of traditional methodologies. In short, the message of *A Nation at Risk* was "Continue your current practice only do it better," e.g., increase high school graduation requirements. Since 1983 other reports have echoed the same message. Although George Bush's *America 2000* did acknowledge the need to challenge some of the assumptions related to the physical structures of education — e.g., length of the school year and the configuration of the school day — it fell far short of calling for the kind of comprehensive restructuring that is necessary for substantive change. Specifically *America 2000* left intact the basic conceptual framework of psychological and epistemological assumptions that have shaped education in America for most of its history.

To say that the problem facing educational reformers is structural is to suggest that the problem is so fundamental that no piecemeal strategy will be sufficient. Once a new educational mission is identified, it will be necessary to design a new structure based on a conceptual framework appropriate to the mission. For example, it should be clear to even the most naive that the knowledge and skills needed for "learning how to learn" are radically different from those that are necessary to achieve education's traditional outcomes, e.g., good grades on standardized tests. And yet our national reports seem to think otherwise. While we would all agree with the need for "A Learning Society ... that affords all members the opportunity to stretch their minds to full capacity, from early childhood through adulthood...," few would argue that this expansive goal can be achieved in a system where, in the words of one 15-year-old, "Schools are designed to teach you to take life sitting down. They prepare you to work in office buildings, to sit in rows or cubicles, to be on time, not to talk back, and to let somebody else grade you" (Keen 1991).

Outdated Assumptions

Education will not change substantively as long as the underlying assumptions that have shaped educational theory and practice for most of this century remain unquestioned and unexamined by most educators. Based on what still goes on in one form or another in many classrooms, most teachers still believe that the essence of good teaching is the passing on of information from a teacher to a student who passively accepts, memorizes, and reproduces on worksheets and tests what the teacher deems to be important. In most classrooms, the model students are those who listen quietly, take appropriate notes, and feed back the expected answer when asked by the teacher. This was brought home to me recently when I presented a "demonstration class" to a group of fifth grade students. My purpose was to demonstrate for observing teachers how provocative questions might trigger creative and imaginative thinking. In the context of an environmental focus, I asked a series of open-ended, metaphorical questions like, "How is the Earth like a washing machine? a suitcase? a book?" During the discussion that followed the presentation, the teacher in whose class I had conducted the demonstration remarked, "What struck me was that the children who responded to your questions were not the same ones who always respond to my questions." I wasn't surprised but wondered if she had really gotten the point.

This suggests that in spite of the rhetoric of national reports and the thousands of new mission statements that these reports triggered, there is a profound disconnect in most of our schools between what organizational theorist Chris Argyris calls "espoused theories" and "theories-in-use." In education, as in other arenas in our culture, our "theories-in-use" are so ingrained that they are seldom examined, precisely because they "remain unconscious and therefore uncritical, concepts … which we take for granted without realizing that we do" (Osborne 1970).

When one examines the assumptions that drive education — not what educators profess to believe (their "espoused theories"), but what actually goes on in most classrooms (their theories-in-use") — it is clear where the difficulty lies. These tacit assumptions cover the entire spectrum of educational practice. They include assumptions about human nature and human potential, assumptions about the nature of knowledge and the way knowledge is acquired, assumptions about intelligence, thinking and learning, and, congruent with these, cultural assumptions about the purposes and goals of education. Together these assumptions make up our mental models. These mental constructs reflect the shared worldview that helps us make sense of the world and thus determine our actions. Scott Peck (1987) refers to these mental models as "rules of the game" and points out that "it is not impractical to consider changing the rules of the game when the game is killing you."

If there is to be substantive educational reform, it must begin with an exploration of these fundamental assumptions. As Chet Bowers (1993) points out, it is necessary to acknowledge that the old rules are no longer effective.

> When traditional practices and beliefs are made explicit, a period of conceptual openness is created that allows for new definitions and relationships to be established. This process involves naming old practices and beliefs in new ways, and then establishing a basis of authority for the newly constituted way of thinking. By this process traditions are modified, renewed, and in some instances, totally discarded.

In sum, the first step in any change process is to become aware of what has been taken for granted for so long. This process, which Charles Tart calls "waking up," is at times difficult, if not impossible, because it is hard for us to even conceptualize any alternative. An examination of these assumptions will make my point clear.

Joseph Chilton Pearce (1980) identifies what may be the most pernicious of all these assumptions. He writes, "We have a cultural notion that if children were not engineered, if we did not manipulate them, they would grow up as beasts in the field." While most parents and teachers would react with discomfort to such a statement, when we consider what goes on in school — and, not so incidently, in many homes — the truth of his statement is obvious.

Closely akin to and emerging from this very fundamental assumption about human nature are others which, though seldom verbalized are reflected in what actually happens in many, probably most, classrooms. For example, the assumptions that

- Children won't learn unless you make them.

- Children can't be trusted to learn on their own.

- Children cannot make intelligent decisions related to their education.

- Only some children are educable.

- All children learn the same way and have similar rates of learning.

- Intelligence is a limited, fixed amount that can be accurately measured with a mathematical formula.

- Intelligence can be defined and measured exclusively in terms of mathematical and verbal skills.

- The ability to remember and recall is a valid measure of intelligence and a good predictor of success.

- Learning is the retention of facts.

- Learning efficiency equals learning effectiveness.

- Teachers know best what is good for children to learn.

- The only way of knowing, i.e., acquiring knowledge, is through our physical senses.

- Each body of knowledge is a distinct and separate "subject" composed of objective, undeniable facts that can be transmitted by teachers talking to students.

Of course, the great irony is that few if any educators profess belief in these. Once while I was presenting this list to a large audience of high school teachers, I was interrupted by an angry voice that literally shouted at me: "You don't think any of *us* believe those, do you?" While educators may indeed profess that they do not accept these assumptions, it is clear to anyone who observes what goes on in schools today that they continue to shape current educational practice.

One thing can be said about these assumptions. They are internally consistent. This is because each reflects a depersonalized, antihuman, empirical perspective that has its roots deep in Western culture and has been a major factor in our perception and treatment of children since the founding of our nation. Even today, in spite of the insights of modern psychology, the viewpoint that "children are little animals" or "children must be seen and not heard" is used by many well-meaning parents to justify harsh and abusive discipline.

The Technological Worldview

This view of human nature is based on an even more fundamental assumption about the nature of reality — an ontological assumption that philosophers call a first principle. A survey of Western intellectual history from Socrates to the present reveals a long history of what today are called paradigm shifts — shifts in the fundamental assumptions, first principles, and subsequent mental models that shape the thinking and action of a culture, i.e., its worldview. Tarnas (1991) points out that beginning in the sixteenth century with the work of Copernicus and Galileo, "a new mental world" was forged "in which old patterns of thinking, traditional prejudices, subjective distortions, verbal confusions, and general intellectual blindness would be overcome by a new (empirical and rational) method of acquiring knowledge." During the next century, based on the work of Newton, Descartes, Bacon, and Darwin, a radically new view of the universe and man's place in it gradually emerged. This new paradigm established a new first principle — namely that "the ... universe was an impersonal phenomenon, governed by regular natural laws, and understandable in exclusively physical and mathematical terms." Newton's metaphor for the universe — a clock — provided a mental model that gave shape to this impersonal, mechanistic worldview, in which "the structure and movement of nature was an entirely secular phenomenon ... the result of an amoral, random, and brutal struggle for survival" (Tarnas 1991). For sake of clarity, I will refer to this perspective as the *technological worldview*. One of the significant consequences of this worldview is that a conceptual split between man and nature was created, which continues even today. In short, nature became the enemy to be conquered.

Closely associated with the technological worldview is the scientific method. Empirical, rational, analytical, atomistic, and linear, this powerful methodology soon became the single acceptable criterion for acquiring knowledge and defining reality. Based on this pragmatic approach, scientists and, in time, lay persons as well, came to assume that reality actually was the way science has described it: a set of irreducible building blocks each of which could be characterized by its precise definition and empirical description. In short, the map, i.e., the scientific method, became identified with the territory, i.e., the world it sought to define and describe. In the words of biophysicist Beverly Rubik (1994), "What began as a method of inquiry was, in time, elevated to an ontology and an epistemology." Acknowledging the impact of this confusion on our entire culture, physicist Frank Tipler suggests that we have become "ontological reductionists." It is as though the world was a fragmented and random collection of jigsaw puzzle pieces. In order to survive, each of us strives to gather together as many pieces as possible. I think of this as *an assumption of separateness*. The mindset based on this assumption has shaped and dominated education during most of the last century and is still the most prevalent perspective in schools today where getting an education is like trying to put together an ever-expanding jigsaw puzzle. Students spend years collecting and sorting pieces of the puzzle. But without some picture to aid their understanding, the pieces they have collected are essentially meaningless and, therefore, useless.

In order to understand the technological worldview, it is necessary to place it in historical perspective. This radically new way of thinking about and understanding our world played a central role in leading Western civilization on the long journey from the Middle Ages into the modern era. Because of its pragmatic power, humans no longer had to depend on traditional authority to tell them what to believe. With the Renaissance and the subsequent Scientific Revolution, people discovered the intellectual tools to acquire for themselves knowledge based on natural, rather than supernatural, explanations for universal processes. In time, "verifiable facts and theories tested and discussed among equals replaced dogmatic revelation hierarchically imposed by an institutional Church" (Tarnas 1991).

American Education has always reflected the technological worldview with its conceptual framework rooted in Newtonian-Cartesian science. Faced with challenges of geographic and industrial expansion, public education was designed with two goals in mind: to Americanize the immigrants who flocked to our shores and to provide industry with a skilled workforce. What better way to train children to sit in rows or cubicles, to be on time, not to talk back, and to let somebody else grade you than to design schools that resembled the factories in which those children would someday work. And, of course, it was a highly successful model. However, as organizational theorist Stan Davis (1979) argues, "Just as farms were not appropriate models for factories, neither are factories appropriate models for information age organizations." In short, the old models have outlived

their usefulness. The time has come to design new models that are relevant
to the needs of the twenty-first rather than the nineteenth century.

The Educational Needs of the Twenty-First Century

An important step in designing new educational models is to identify
the desired outcomes — that is, the knowledge and skills that today's
students will need to succeed in the next century. To determine exactly what
those skills might be requires a rigorous analysis of the real world — a
world that has changed dramatically in the last 50 years. Indeed, these
changes have been so profound that although many in our society are still
pursuing the post-World War II American Dream, there now appears to be
a fundamental disconnect between the assumptions upon which that
dream was based and the harsh realities that face today's high school and
college graduates. While we should be preparing students for life in the
twenty-first century, we are actually educating them to live in the "good old
days" of the mid-twentieth century. This incongruence between the dream
and the reality has resulted in a series of anomalies that are harbingers of
even more potentially devastating disconnects to come. The reality is that:

- There is no longer a guaranteed job waiting for every high school
  or college graduate. An increasing number of available jobs are
  low-paying positions for which many graduates are overquali-
  fied.

- An increasing number of better-paying jobs, e.g., Robert Reich's
  (1992) "symbolic analysts," require skills that aren't learned by
  most students in most schools.

- There is no longer the promise of a better standard of living for
  each succeeding generation. Indeed, the reverse is more often the
  case.

- Our institutions are either not working, e.g., government, or are
  changing rapidly as traditional organizational structures and
  management strategies become increasingly counterproductive.

- There is no longer a consensus on the fundamental values that
  shape our national character and guide our personal lives. Issues

that seemed clear and unambiguous for most of our parents now threaten the very fabric of our society.

- There seems to be a loss of vision and lack of will on the part of ordinary citizens. As people feel ever more powerless, individually and collectively we seem to have become a nation of victims who have little, if any, apparent control over our lives.

The truth, often hidden under layers of political rhetoric, is that everything is coming unglued. The assumptions that have held our world together for the last 50 years — assumptions that every American could take for granted — are no longer valid. Violence, crime, drug abuse, child abuse, famine, and war are merely symptoms of a far more fundamental incongruity between the dream and the reality.

But there is more. Although many still wish to define our "national interest" in narrow, parochial, self-serving terms, the reality is otherwise. As *A Nation at Risk* observed, "The world is indeed one global village." And, whether we want to acknowledge it or not, the problems and issues we face at the national level are reflected globally where future generations will be confronted with profound and universal dilemmas that, at the present time, seem to be intransigent. These dilemmas, and their relevance to the goals of education, can no longer be ignored.

1. Destruction of the planetary ecological systems. Of all the dilemmas this is the most threatening precisely because if the planet's ecological systems break down, no one can survive. Although at a rational level most people would accept this fact, we continue to take our natural world for granted , in spite of all the warning signals. And yet these planetary life support systems are as fragile and as essential to human survival as the air tanks carried on the backs of scuba divers. When they stop functioning survival is impossible.

2. Population growth and limited resources/resource depletion. The potential breakdown of ecological systems is exacerbated by human population growth and the competition for increasingly scarce resources. Today world population is growing exponentially while the natural resources on which we humans are dependent are at best stable, but more often diminishing at alarming rates — usually as the consequence of applied technology that is the hallmark of Western culture.

3. *The economic imparity between the "haves" and the "have-nots."* Lester Brown and his colleagues at Worldwatch Institute have concluded that of all the principal driving forces that have contributed directly to the excessive pressures on the earth's natural systems, the growing inequality in income between rich and poor stands out in sharpest relief. "This chasm of inequity … fosters over-consumption at the top of the ladder and persistent poverty at the bottom."

4. *The vulnerability of technological systems.* Western nations are increasingly saddled with the fiscal nightmare of trying to maintain their highly sophisticated technological infrastructures. For example, it has been estimated it will cost more than the present three trillion dollar national debt just to *restore to maintenance level* our highways, bridges, public buildings, power lines, and public transportation systems. In addition, our centralized national infrastructures are highly vulnerable to both terrorist attacks and natural disasters. Ironically, in spite of a hundred years of channeling, dredging, damming, and diking by the Army Corps of Engineers, in a few short weeks the Mississippi River effectively demonstrated the limitations of human hubris.

5. *Genocide/arms race/nuclear war.* Lester Brown (1994) notes that "during 40 years of East-West confrontation, government planners seemed prepared for every possible scenario and braced for every contingency save one: the end of the cold war." One consequence is that the arms race goes on unabated. While the growth of nuclear weapons has lessened considerably, now small nations and often their racial or ethnic minorities attempt to emulate large nations by arming themselves to the teeth. Within our own country neighbors and even entire neighborhoods are trapped in their own arms races.

Genocide neither began nor ended with the Holocaust. Since World War II, it has continued virtually unabated in Cambodia and is evident in former Yugoslavia and in the Rwandan Civil War where entire tribes were literally threatened with extinction. Roger Winter (1994), director of the U.S. Committee for Refugees writes, "Go deep inside Rwanda today and you

will not find gas chambers or massive crematoria. But you will find genocide ... eerily reminiscent of the 'Final Solution' attempted 50 years ago."

6. *The failure of political action at a global level.* Ultimately, the ability to
address the dilemmas identified above is dependent upon the willingness
of nations — reflecting the intention and commitment of their citizens — to
both individually and collectively take positive and aggressive corrective
action. Yet, in face of these overarching issues, the political capacities of
governmental agencies seems trapped in gridlock.

7. *The breakdown of community.* Shaped by the atomistic perspective
of the Scientific Revolution, our modern society operates on the assumption
that the individual is the fundamental social unit — the "basic building
block" — of human society. The reality is quite different. Until quite recently in Western culture, it was recognized that the community — the
neighborhood, extended family, clan, or tribe — provided the crucial
social cohesion that is so necessary for an individual's physical protection,
social well-being, and emotional health.

The deterioration of community that has taken place in our own
country during the last 50 years, is now taking place worldwide. As a result
of the pervasive economic imperialism of the West, community is being
replaced by a universal market that is very expensive in human terms. "The
unification of the market goes hand in hand with the fragmentation of
culture" (Lasch 1995).

8. *The lack of vision and the loss of will on the part of ordinary citizens.* One
byproduct of the loss of community has been the diminution of personal
power. Yet, until ordinary citizens decide that they can make a difference,
neither nations nor global organizations like the United Nations can act
decisively to address the crises that humanity faces. As they are now
organized, political and economic systems are hierarchial and serve primarily the interests of those who have a stake in maintaining the status quo.
Even in democracies, elections reflect little more than a change in the faces
of those in power.

Conclusion

Education, as it is presently structured, is simply not capable of preparing students to face the real issues that will have most impact on their futures, *primarily because outdated assumptions that have driven educational theory and practice for most of the twentieth century are no longer relevant to the real world.* Organizational consultant Joel Barker (1990) states the case succinctly: "The solutions to the future lie outside the boundaries of our present assumptions about the way we do things."

This suggests that if our children and grandchildren are to have any hope of living in a better, safer, happier world, their education must be based on a different set of assumptions — assumptions that are appropriate to the realities of the world as it is today. The rest of this book is designed to aid in this task.

Chapter Two

The Design Solution: Systems Thinking

The great ... issues of our times have to do in one way or another with our failure to see things in their entirety. That failure occurs when minds are taught to think in boxes and not taught to transcend those boxes or to question overly much how they fit with other boxes. (David Orr)

Schools that teach children to take life sitting down simply are not preparing them for life in the 21st century. If students are to acquire the insights, knowledge, and skills needed for personal success and social survival, we will have to completely redesign education. Toward this end, we must not only examine the assumptions that shape current educational policy and practice, but also identify and explore new assumptions that are both appropriate to the desired outcomes and, at the same time, realistic, reasonable, and practical. These assumptions must have a solid foundation — ideally a combination of research, experience, intuition, and insight. Fortunately, there are a number of such assumptions about human nature and human potential, the nature of knowledge, intelligence, thinking and learning, and, at a more fundamental level, the nature of the universe and our relationship to it, which have emerged from research in many fields, including physics, anthropology, psychology, and semantics. Ironically, many of these have been the "espoused theories" of leading educators for more than a decade. But most have a much more ancient lineage, having shaped human thinking and behavior in indigenous cultures for thousands of years. Indeed, they are often implicit in the language we use. For example, the Latin root word *educare* from which our word education is derived, means literally *to draw forth*. The obvious assumption is that there is an unrealized potential within each of us that can be drawn forth. This was, of course, the assumption upon which the Socratic dialogue — often considered the epitome of good educational practice — was based. Even though these assumptions have not been manifest in mainstream education, most of us intuitively accept their validity.

Assumptions About Human Nature

Seventy-five years ago Alfred North Whitehead (1957) stated what should be obvious.

> Students are alive, and the purpose of education is to stimulate and guide their self-development. It follows as a corollary from this premise that the teachers also should be alive with living thoughts.

More recently, early childhood educator Katharine Kersey (1983) suggested a powerful metaphor that carries with it a set of assumptions about education that have the potential for literally transforming educational practice.

> Children are given to us — on loan — for a very short period of time. They come to us like packets of flower seeds, with no pictures on the cover and no guarantees. We do not know what they will look like, be like, act like, or have the potential to become.
>
> Our job, like the gardener's, is to meet their needs as best we can: to give proper nourishment, love, attention, and caring, and to hope for the best. The gardener learns to be "tuned into" the plant.

Implicit in this perspective is the assumption of an innate human potential far beyond the bounds of traditional thinking. Just as every acorn has the potential to become a mighty oak, all children have a unmeasurable potential to be fully human. In short, with the obvious exception of brain damage, every child is born with a wide range of potentials that we have only just begun to understand.

For example, Michael Murphy, in his recent book *The Future of the Body*

(1992), focuses on what Jean Houston calls "the possible human." Studying the oral and written histories of many cultures, Murphy sought evidence of extraordinary physical, mental, and spiritual capacities in areas such as metanormal perception, cognition, movement, vitality, and spiritual development. Recognizing the necessity to "reject scientific, religious, and other prejudices against certain time-tested data from (non-conventional) traditions," he explores such unorthodox sources as the contemplative traditions, anthropological studies of shamanism, and psychical research. Murphy also explores the extensive literature that has emerged from the physical, biological, and human sciences, and new fields such as psychoneuroimmunology. He concludes:

> Taken in its entirety, the material presented in this book suggests that human nature harbors extraordinary attributes that may appear in sickness, healing, or programs for growth, either spontaneously or through formal discipline. While such attributes require long-term cultivation for their fullest development, they frequently appear to be freely given, sometimes when we do not seek or expect them. (1992)

If Murphy accurately assesses human possibilities, we can no longer afford to limit our understanding of human potential to the assumptions that presently shape our educational system. As every parent intuitively knows, while current assumptions may contain partial truths, they are not adequate to explain the incalculable mystery, beauty, and elegance of a newborn infant. In spite of traditional science's claim of a mechanistic universe, we all know that children simply cannot be reduced to materialistic dimensions. Caring parents intuitively recognize that their children represent a potential that can only be anticipated — call it life, spirit, consciousness, or as the ancient Hebrews termed it, breath. Refer to it as will, thought, or mind. However we define this potential, we must acknowledge that it exists and that it reflects the mysterious, unknowable elements of existence that cannot be reduced to quantifiable physical matter.

Thus, before we can design a new structure for education, it is necessary to identify those alternative assumptions that can guide and shape educational transformation. As I have indicated, most of them are self-evident to parents and teachers. Because these are things we know but don't know we know, it is necessary to *educate* ourselves by *calling them forth* out of our own intuitive wisdom.

Assumptions About the Nature of the Universe

As noted in Chapter 1, our assumptions about human nature reflect even more fundamental assumptions — first principles — about the nature of the universe. In the first chapter I identified an *"assumption of separateness"* as the first principle that gave shape to the technological worldview and all of our Western institutions including education. This perspective is fragmented, impersonal, random, and mechanistic. In contrast, the assumptions discussed above reflect a radically different worldview based on an *"assumption of wholeness."* This assumption holds that at some fundamental level of reality, *everything is connected to everything else.* Supported by the Theory of Relativity, quantum physics, chaos theory, and ecology, this worldview — which I call the *"ecological worldview"* — has only recently emerged into public consciousness, having received pragmatic validity and renewed vitality from the photographs of Earth taken from space. However, its roots are deep in the intuitive wisdom of humankind and are evident in all of the world's religions and indigenous cultures. Even as the earliest human experiences recognized a fundamental dualism implicit in the nature of things — yin/yang, you/me, right/left, light/dark — it was also recognized that these dualisms were grounded in a primal wholeness. This perspective is explicit in what is often referred to as "The Perennial Wisdom" of humankind. This was not a philosophical position that our primal ancestors arrived at intellectually. Rather it emerged from their experiential and intuitive knowledge of a profound relationship of connectedness to the Earth and all living things. It was not until the scientific revolution that duality emerged as the defining characteristic of the universe. In short, this unitive worldview is not new. The relevance of this holistic perspective to education was made explicit in a report of the Carnegie Foundation for the Advancement of Teaching (Boyer and Levine n.d.) almost 20 years ago. The report stated the case succinctly: "The goal of common learning is to understand the 'connectedness of things.' " To achieve this goal, however, educators must embrace a radically different understanding not only of human nature, but of the nature of knowledge, intelligence, thinking and learning as well.

It should be no surprise to find that the scientific method with its powerful array of analytical tools soon reduced the entire world into a virtually infinite assortment of discrete facts, each with its carefully crafted, precise definition. In education, concepts like knowledge, intelligence, thinking, and learning were defined in quantifiable terms designed to satisfy the empirical requirements of a culture firmly committed to the technological worldview. Knowledge was reduced to the accumulation of facts; intelligence was defined as a fixed, mathematically measurable capacity for linear, sequential verbal, and mathematical abilities; thinking was considered to be the function of an identifiable set of discrete cognitive tools, e.g., Bloom's Taxonomy; and learning was universally thought of in terms of memory and recall. While educational policy and practice based on these theoretical constructs fostered the kind of knowledge and skills that were valued by a rapidly expanding industrial society, as is evident from the current failures of our educational system and by the crises which face Western culture, this kind of education is no longer relevant to the real world. However, before we can comprehend the magnitude of the shift in thinking that must take place, it is important to understand both the current perspective, shaped as it was by the theories of eighteenth and nineteenth century science, and the emerging perspective that is being shaped by new theories in both the natural and behavioral sciences.

Because of its analytical, reductionist methodology, Willis Harman (1988) has called Newtonian/Cartesian science a "science of the parts." Without discounting its value, Harman argues convincingly that, as a result of relativity theory, quantum mechanics, and ecology, what is rapidly emerging today is a "science of whole systems" — a science that is complementary to rather than competitive with a science of the parts. With its focus on the big picture, systems science provides an important and necessary context for understanding and applying traditional science's analytical expertise. Obviously, the two methodologies are based on different assumptions and models about the nature of the world. With the machine as its guiding metaphor, Newtonian science is based on certain theoretical assumptions that are materialistic and mechanistic in character. While there are many natural laws that have quantifiable, machinelike qualities, e.g., laws of motion, the mechanistic metaphor is no longer sufficient to represent our expanding knowledge of the universe. It should come as no surprise to find that the guiding metaphor for systems science is the organism. The theoretical foundation for this science of whole systems is known as the Theory of Living Systems. Just as analytical thinking is the primary cognitive strategy for understanding the parts, so systems thinking is the primary cognitive strategy for understanding systems as unified wholes.

The Assumptions of the Scientific Method

It is important to see analytical thinking and systems thinking as complementary rather than contradictory or oppositional ways of thinking. Each of them has several defining characteristics that can help us understand their power, their relevance, and their limitations. Because analytical thinking is fundamental to the scientific method, we will explore some of the implications implicit in the methodology.

The methodology of science assumes a mechanical universe. Descartes' greatest legacy was surely the mechanistic philosophy. From this philosophical base, it was a logical step to the notion that the universe, consisting of matter and motion, was a vast machine — Newton's clock — wound up by God to tick forever. All nonmaterial phenomena ultimately have a material basis and thus can be explained empirically. It didn't take long for men — and it was a male-dominated era — to design an economic system that ran like clockwork with humans perceived and treated as interchangeable cogs in a great industrial machine. As science learned more about the human body, it, too, came to be understood and treated as a machine composed of pumps, bellows, levers, and valves. The obvious consequence was, in time, a radical transformation of every facet of human culture — a transformation based on the assumption that we inhabit an inert, dead planet in an inert, random universe.

Four methodological characteristics are implicit in the scientific method: (a) It is reductionist and atomistic; (b) it is rational, pragmatic, and empirical; (c) it assumes objectivity; and (d) it assumes an either/or logic.

The methodology of science is reductionist and atomistic. As has already been noted, the scientific method is analytical in nature. Because things, problems, and knowledge itself are complex by nature, in order to understand them, they must be broken down into their simplest discrete component parts. Once these parts have been comprehended, then, using logical, sequential steps, they can then be incrementally reassembled into the whole. Facts, then, are considered to be building blocks of knowledge — the basic "stuff" out of which ideas, concepts, and knowledge can be incrementally created. Implicit in this methodology are the assumptions that *meaning is inherent in the self-evident parts* and that *the whole is equal to a sum of its parts.* Larger meanings can be discovered only by first understanding the parts and then reconstructing the whole.

The methodology of science is rational, pragmatic, and empirical. Rationalism is the belief that human reason, based on observation and common sense, is the primary source of our knowledge of the world. This obviously highly practical approach gave birth to a philosophical position called positivism. Positivism provided the major theme of the scientific revolution, namely that "Our goal is how, not why." Science historian Morris Berman (1984) summarized Newton's conclusion. "That I cannot explain gravity is irrelevant. I can measure it, observe it, make predictions based on it, and this is all the scientist has to do."

The methodology assumes objectivity. Because reality is fixed and absolute, it is possible to completely separate the observer from that which is being observed and measured. Objective research is based on the assumption that two people observing or measuring the same phenomenon will agree on details concerning the object of their investigation. Thus, the only way to eliminate bias and other value-laden, subjective qualities from research is by the appropriate application of the scientific method.

The methodology assumes an "either/or" logic based on the Aristotelian principle of noncontradiction. Aristotle argued that a "thing cannot both be and not be at the same time." This led to the creation of distinctions such as living/nonliving. While these distinctions appropriately established the differences between things *by definition,* in time these same definitions came to be accepted as reality itself.

Power, Relevance, and Limitations of the Scientific Method

The power and value of the scientific method is obvious. It has provided us with all of the technological advantages of modernity and made it possible for us to gain significant insights into the way things work. By recognizing that both the smallest and the largest objects in the universe obey identical laws, we have learned with a fairly high level of accuracy to predict, and thus anticipate events such as earthquakes, volcanoes, and hurricanes.

Equally obvious, however, is that this methodology has its limitations. There are times when even its staunchest protagonists must wonder whether some of the results of science and technology are not consequences of some "Faustian bargain." As a consequence of its "assumed to be value-neutral" methodology, our home planet has become just another object to be manipulated and shaped to human size. This has resulted in what Morris Berman (1984) calls a profound "disenchantment of the world." In his words, because of its "rigid distinction between observer and observed, scientific consciousness is alienated consciousness.... I am an alienated 'thing' in a world of other, equally meaningless things."

A third limitation is that the methodology encourages an inflexible, literalistic interpretation of the universe. The tendency of the scientific method to define reality in precise, concrete terms that carry the aura of absolute certainty has led to the conclusion — to use Korsybski's term, that "the map *is* the territory" — that the universe is the way science has described it. For example, most educated people today seem to forget that the Big Bang Theory is still only a theory. There is not, nor ever can be, empirical, observable data that will prove or disprove the theory. In short, although this theoretical construct is internally consistent with the scientific description of the universe, it is not necessarily true in any ontological sense. This emphasis on words and their meaning based on "concrete knowledge of facts" is called *nominalism* — a philosophical perspective that defines the nature of reality in its own terms. This philosophical view has had a particularly powerful and pernicious influence in the social sciences in which empiricism is not as self-evident as in the physical sciences. One can measure and quantify electricity, but before one can measure a concept like intelligence, it is first necessary to define the concept, to reduce it to terms that are quantifiable. While such strategies have been useful in the past, they are becoming increasingly limiting and counterproductive.

Finally, and this may be its predominant limitation, in the analytical process the big picture of the whole gets lost: "You can't see the forest because of the trees." While there is nothing wrong with studying only trees, it is impossible to really understand the nature of trees without some insight as to the nature of the forest.

It goes without saying that in spite of its inherent limitations and outdated assumptions about the nature of the universe, this technological worldview continues to dominates educational practice. It should be equally clear, as Einstein observed more than half a century ago, "The world we have made as a result of the level of thinking we have done thus far creates problems we cannot solve at the same level of thinking. With the splitting of the atom, everything has changed but man's thinking."

The Systems View

There is another way of thinking that, because it is comprehensive, incorporates rather than replaces the analytical mode. It is generally called systems thinking and has, during the last decade, given rise to a different kind of science — a science of whole systems known as systems science. Systems science is based on the Theory of Living Systems and provides scientists with a wide variety of increasingly rigorous methodologies with which to study and more accurately predict the behavior of complex systems, e.g., the weather or a forest ecosystem. Because their focus is on the forest as an integrated *system* of relationships, rather than on the trees as separate entities, these methodologies lack the precision of analytical tools. On the other hand, they provide us with a more comprehensive understanding about the trees and the relationships that exist among them. To suggest that one perspective is truer or better than the other is like arguing that the perspective of the microscope is more true or better than the perspective of the telescope. Each provides important and necessary information about the nature of reality without which any insight, understanding, or knowledge is incomplete, biased, and fundamentally inaccurate. With the emergence of a vigorous systems science, the important thing is to know how these two complementary perspectives can be used for maximum insight, knowledge, and effectiveness.

This perspective reinforces the intuitive insight that *no single, discrete entity can be fully understood apart from the complex whole of which it is an integral part.* The whole provides the context without which our knowledge of the part is necessarily limited. For example, although a tree can be described with detailed precision, our understanding of the tree is severely limited unless we can study it in the context of its habitat — the forest or meadow ecosystem to which it belongs. This same contextual principle applies to our understanding of concepts like intelligence. Although we may define and describe intelligence in explicit terms, there is no way one can understand intelligence in isolation from a thinking and learning human organism. In short, systems thinking is contextual thinking because it recognizes that without a context, meaning is truncated and incomplete.

There are several characteristics of systems thinking that help distinguish it from analytical thinking: (a) It incorporates a both/and logic; (b) it assumes a living universe; (c) it values ecological thinking; (d) it recognizes that we live in a participatory universe; (e) it is at the same time both local and global; and (f) it honors the long-range view.

Systems thinking incorporates a both/and rather than an either/or logic. Analytical thinking is by its very nature an either/or process. By including one thing, its logic excludes another. Because systems thinking provides the big, comprehensive perspective, its logic is inclusive and integrative based on both/and thinking. In short, systems thinking unites opposites, honors diversity, and acknowledges differences, e.g., it respects the value of analytical detail. Because it is comprehensive, this way of thinking is generative and suggests new perspectives, new insights, and new ways of organizing information to achieve optimal outcomes. For example, while the systemic perspective recognizes the value of the scientific method and the benefits that have been derived from its technological accomplishments, it simultaneously honors the age-old wisdom and values that shaped human communities from the beginning. By combining these perspectives, we can design technologies that support human values and benefit, rather than destroy, the social bonds that maintain communities and stabilize cultures. Just as cross-country travelers need both local street maps and larger state maps to successfully arrive at their destinations, so we will need all of our cognitive resources — analysis and systemic — to address the multiple dilemmas that confront human societies at the planetary level.

Systems thinking assumes a living universe. In contrast to the lifeless machine, the metaphor that best represents the systems view of the world is the organism. This is most adequately embodied in the Gaia Hypothesis, which "considers earth as a living organism and humanity as its unfolding network of consciousness" (Schaer 1988). This organic metaphor and the Theory of Living Systems upon which it is based, suggests that all of the planet's subsystems, both ecological and cultural, e.g., social, economic, and political systems, are also self-regulating, self-organizing living systems. At a macro-level, this metaphor also suggests that the universe itself may be a living system. While this is no more provable than the Big Bang Theory, it does reflect the internal consistency of the theory.

Systems thinking is ecological thinking. Because the Earth's ecological systems are authentic and practical models of living systems, what we know about how ecological systems function provides us with the best and most comprehensive understanding of how other living systems function. Thus, to understand the principles of ecology is to understand the principles of all living systems. Systems thinking, then, is applying these principles to increase our understanding of how cultural, economic, political, and organizational systems can be designed to function more effectively. This is why the emerging view is often called the ecological worldview.

Systems thinking recognizes that we live in a participatory universe. As we now know from even a cursory knowledge of quantum physics, the observer is always and unavoidably an influential part of every experiment. This, of course, disproves the notion that science is, or can be, objective. We are forced to acknowledge that all human experience, including so-called "objective" knowledge, is at some profoundly elemental level subjective in nature. This means that rather than being *discoverers* of objective knowledge, we are *creators* of knowledge — knowledge that always reflects the subjective perspectives of those who create it.

Systems thinking is both global and, at the same time, local. The essence of systems thinking is captured in the ubiquitous phrase, "think globally, act locally." This is the insight that *whatever influences a part of any system has an impact on the entire system* — the so-called "butterfly effect." Whether one is talking about butterflies and weather, the impact of DDT sprayed locally on global ecological systems, or the impact of political turmoil in a single country on the global economy, decisions made locally will *always* influence the whole, and therefore, must be made within that context. If we are consistent in our interpretation of systems theory, we must also conclude that every action that I take makes a difference on the entire system. In short, to quote ecologist Garrett Hardin, "You can never do just one thing." Mary Catherine Bateson (1994) points out, from a systems perspective, "the spotted owl stands for the preservation of an entire ecosystem." According to the ecological worldview, this kind of insight is ordinary common sense. In short, the entire Earth is our backyard! To think otherwise is like trying to drill a hole in one end of a crowded lifeboat and expecting the other end to remain afloat.

Systems thinking honors the long-range view. The Native American practice of making decisions in the context of "the seventh generation" is a pragmatic example of systems thinking. Because of its long-range perspective, systems thinking makes it easier to anticipate and thus address problems before they arise rather than waiting until they have happened and, one by one, attempt to solve them. Once we acknowledge the need for a long-range perspective, we can design the mechanisms by which a future goal is to be achieved.

Power, Relevance, and Limitations of Systems Thinking

In sum, the power, value, and relevance of systems thinking lies in the fact that systems science provides us with context — the big picture — without which the details, no matter how precise, can easily mislead us in our search for explanations. By making it possible to differentiate between anomalies and perturbations that are symptomatic of more fundamental disorders, and those that are inherent in the system, the big picture enables us to address the inherent disease rather than merely treat the symptoms. As the methodologies of system science become more sophisticated, its predictive power will become more powerful. Problems can be anticipated before they occur, making possible alternatives, e.g., evacuation prior to hurricanes, which were not previously available. Finally, systems thinking is a powerful tool for learning how to learn, that is, knowing how to get what one needs to know when it is needed. By providing the big picture, it enables one to select, organize, and apply only information that is relevant to a particular situation.

Systems thinking also has its limitations, the primary one being that it does not provide the kind of detail that is often required to "fix" something. For example, while systems thinking enables us to predict the potential ecological breakdown of a large body of water, e.g., Lake Erie, without the detailed knowledge of pollutants and their effect provided by a science of the parts, even relatively short-term rehabilitation would be impossible.

It becomes clear that both analytical thinking and systems thinking are complementary capacities. As I have noted, the real skill is learning how they can best be used together to create a sane, healthy world for all living things.

Systems Thinking and Intelligence, Thinking, and Learning

During the last 30 years, research in humanistic psychology, cognitive science, and pedagogy has provided significant new insights into the nature of intelligence, thinking, and learning. What has become clear is that what I have called systems thinking is more than just an alternative mode of thought. It is the natural, holistic way of thinking that is innate in humans. It doesn't need to be taught. Indeed, it can't be. It can only be nurtured. At the present, for many people, it is no more than a potential which, like a seed hidden in a cave, has lain dormant waiting for its time. The challenge facing educators today is to recognize that there is an enormous unrealized potential that is inherent in every child and to redesign educational practice so that schools nurture rather than destroy this potential.

Since education is primarily about knowledge, intelligence, thinking, and learning, any fundamental shift in our understanding of these concepts will by necessity lead to profound and even dramatic changes in the way we educate people in our society.

Once educators begin to think systemically, the process of educational transformation will begin in earnest. It already has started in a number of schools and classrooms — like Thompson Middle School (see Introduction). Therefore, it is important that we explore in some depth what systems thinking is and does.

Systems thinking is a natural way of thinking that is integrative. Recent research has established that at what I call *the deep structure of thinking and learning,* these "cognitive" processes involve not only the right and left hemispheres of the neocortex but also, and simultaneously, the intuitive/affective processes associated with the limbic brain *and* the sensory processes associated with the reptilian brain (Ellison 1990). Since these sensory processes reflect input from every cell of the body, we can only conclude that *thinking and learning are integrative, whole-brain, whole-body processes that consist of rational, intuitive, affective, sensory, and volitional ways of knowing.* Indeed, studies suggest that thinking and learning, which on the surface appear to be two separate, albeit related, processes, at a structural level are essentially mirror images of each other. From this perspective, it would be accurate to envision *thinking/learning* as a single, integrated, contextual process with two faces. In all cases, for maximum efficiency and effectiveness, this process requires a gestalt, or big picture, as the context for processing incoming data.

Not only does this integrative structure shape all of the so-called thinking skills, e.g., analysis, synthesis, evaluation, problem-solving, decision-making, it patterns all modes of human learning, such as verbal, mathematical, kinesthetic, spatial. When a mode of thought such as analysis is limited to linear, sequential methodologies, as in the scientific method, the resulting information provides only a partial, and therefore inaccurate image of reality. While this information may be useful and necessary, it is not, nor ever can be, complete in and of itself. In short, science's image is a reduced image — as it might appear through a keyhole rather than an open door.

In all fairness it is important to recognize that responsible scientific investigators are *contextual thinkers.* Even as they analyse an object or event, they intuitively if not deliberately assume a *whole* as the context for their work. Unfortunately, because the scientific method does not explicitly acknowledge *context* as relevant to an investigation, the conclusions that are reached generally stand alone in grand isolation from the whole to which they belong. Thus, what may be no more than an interesting *correlation* — say between a gene and a particular form of cancer — can easily be interpreted as *casual*, particularly by a lay person.

We cannot really understand the functions we call thinking and learning apart from their relationship to intelligence. Physicist Peter Russell (1983) provides us with a systemic description of intelligence that highlights these functional qualities.

> Intelligence itself is an organizing principle within human consciousness. In its most generalized sense intelligence can be thought of as the ability to abstract raw sensory data, organizing our perceptions into meaningful wholes, form relationships between them (concepts, expectations, hypotheses, etc.), and thereby organize action in a purposeful way.

From this systemic perspective, it seems plausible to suggest that *intelligence, thinking, and learning are inseparable processes.* To be more accurate, *intelligence/thinking/learning is a single, dynamic, multi-faceted, functional capacity that is inherent in human consciousness. This capacity may be expressed in a variety of modes.*

It is not surprising to find a definition of learning that also reflects this conclusion. Australian whole language specialist Brian Cambourne (1989) writes that "Learning is a process that involves making connections, identifying patterns, and organizing previously unrelated bits of knowledge, behavior and action into new patterned wholes. The learner is the one who must make the connections."

Thompson* Special Education teacher Jan Sutfin reflects on what happens when students are encouraged to make their own connections.

> I sincerely doubt that the higher order thinking that took place in that sixth grade, heterogeneously grouped classroom during our year together would have occurred had we still been separating subjects and using the text as our teaching tool. During that year, the students really became the curriculum as their concerns were addressed, their ideas were expressed and as they went home to share "big ideas" with their friends and parents. They also became more open minded and accepting of each other as valuable, responsible human beings. It was quite a year of intellectual growth for all the students which, of course, included my special ones too.

---

* Thompson Middle School in St. Charles, IL., is mentioned frequently in this book and references to teacher's experiences with the integrated curriculum are drawn from there, unless otherwise noted.

Sharon Young, another Special Education teacher at Thompson, comments on the effectiveness of a learner-centered approach. "More meaning is gained when the student makes his own personal connection. When completing a realistic task, my kids can make connections that I wouldn't have considered possible. They can also explain their reasoning."

Because of our reductionist mode of thought — reflected as it is in our language — our understanding of intelligence, thinking, and learning has been confined to precise definitions. The consequence is that we continue to treat them as three, separate, discrete functions connected in a linear, cause-and-effect relationship (intelligence >>> thinking >>> learning).

Though it is necessary and useful at times to consider these as separate functions, it is a fundamental epistemological error to assume that they are indeed separate. Because the understanding of intelligence, thinking, learning, knowledge, and information that dominate most educational practice continues to reflect the assumptions of scientific rationalism, most textbooks, curriculum, and teaching methods perpetuate this fundamental error.

The recognition that intelligence is a dynamic process has led to an explosion of research. Perhaps the best known is the work of Howard Gardner who has investigated the multidimensional nature of intelligence. He has identified seven diverse modes through which intelligence can be expressed (Gardner 1984). In addition to the commonly accepted verbal and mathematical modes, Gardner identifies musical, spatial, kinesthetic, intrapersonal, and interpersonal intelligences. He concludes that, probably, all children have the potential for genius in at least one of these modalities.

What if every student is potentially a genius? What if teachers began each day with the assumption that they had a classroom full of geniuses? What if schools recognized that each of the seven "intelligences" were equally relevant and valued manifestations of human potential?

Systems Thinking and Knowledge

New insights about the nature of intelligence have led to new assumptions about knowledge in general, and specifically about the relationship between knowledge and meaning. The search for meaning is recognized as being fundamental to human nature, and therefore central to the educational process. Based on her crosscultural studies, anthropologist Mary Catherine Bateson (1994) reinforces this perspective. "Humans construct meaning as spiders make webs.... This is how we survive, our primary evolutionary business."

However, just as a piece of a jigsaw puzzle is meaningless apart from the picture, so any given fact or isolated piece of raw data is meaningless apart from some larger context or whole. Meaningful knowledge — which, of course, is what we want to teach in our schools — is contextual knowledge. The essence of contextual knowledge is knowing how to identify, create, and explore contexts of meaning. Thinking contextually is the essence of systems thinking.

This new understanding of the nature of knowledge makes it clear that facts have no intrinsic meaning. Every fact represents a point of view, created and shaped within a specific cultural context and meaningful only within that context. For example, concepts such as sanity, intelligence, or morality are culturally relative and can have no absolute definition.

To appreciate the relationship between knowledge, context, and meaning, it is useful to understand how knowledge is structured. Hilda Taba (1982) has identified four levels of knowledge:

- Thought Systems

- Concepts

- Basic Ideas

- Facts

Conventional curricula are structured inductively, from bottom to top, treating facts as the building blocks of knowledge. Recognizing the role that context plays in thinking and learning, an integrated, learner-centered curriculum will be organized deductively, from top to bottom. It will begin with thought systems — the "big picture" — as a context from which concepts, basic ideas, and facts can be deduced and understood. When a curriculum is organized in this way, students experience using both deductive and inductive thinking/learning processes in an integrated, systemic manner. Because it resonates with the child's natural way of thinking and learning, this way of organizing the curriculum enhances their ability to select, organize, and apply concepts, ideas, and facts in meaningful and creative pursuits.

Thompson eighth grade science teacher Bonnie Pettebone writes of her experience.

> It's the Big Picture. That's what allows kids to really learn. I used to give them one of my great lectures and then turn them loose in the lab to "see" what I had already told them. Now, we start with a couple of weeks of self-paced labs. As the kids go through the labs, the activities do the teaching. It's amazing, they really discover it. They really do understand — so much better than before. Now I'm starting with the entire Periodic Table. This way they get the entire picture and make connections.

The Educational Relevance of Systems Thinking

If the insights noted above are indeed a reflection of the real world, several inescapable conclusions follow.

Systems thinking makes it possible to know more with less information. As the power of science to generate new knowledge about the world increased, the age of the Renaissance Man who presumably "knew it all," came to an end. In his place is the expert — one who "knows more and more about less and less." Unfortunately, when the expert's knowledge is applied without consideration of the context that the Renaissance Man intuitively understood, problems begin to appear, e.g., DDT and ozone depletion.

The expert is the logical product of an educational system that considers facts to be the building blocks of knowledge and organizes teaching and learning so that "the one with the most facts wins!" The highly publicized "world class standards" defended by educators and politicians alike, reflect this outdated perspective. Such an approach is not only destructive to the human potential for creativity and generativity, it has become increasingly impractical in an age in which the growth of information is exponential — in some fields doubling each year. In the same way that the picture of a jigsaw puzzle helps one be selective in searching for pieces, the systems perspective provides a gestalt that enables one to be selective in determining what detailed information is required. In short, we no longer have to "know it all" in order to understand an issue, a problem, or a field of study. We can literally know more with less information — a very powerful ability in an information age.

I have found the following analogy helpful in understanding how this is possible. When we compare the structure of knowledge with the structure of a house, we can make the following associations:

Thought Systems = Blueprints

Concepts = Framing

Basic Ideas = Room Dividers

Facts = Furniture

Thought systems are cognitive blueprints that show how the various concepts, ideas, and facts fit together within a given discipline. Concepts provide the conceptual framework, i.e., mental model, that gives shape and meaning to the thought system. Just as one knows more about a building by understanding its structure than from a pile of lumber, one can know more about a subject by understanding its conceptual structure, that is, the way it is organized. In short, one knows more with less detailed information. It is as simple as the insight that one learns more about a puzzle by spending five minutes studying the picture than by spending hours on sorting and fitting together pieces. In conclusion, *facts are not the building blocks of knowledge.* As Theodore Roszak (1994) observes, "Ideas come first." What he calls "master ideas," like *all men are created equal,* are not derived from some "body of facts" but rather are created by the imagination from experience. These master ideas often become the organizing principles that shape a culture. However, master ideas require living, vital, empirical expression to imbue them with meaning. In the same way, thought systems and conceptual structures need facts as the furniture that provides the detail and specificity, the color and texture, that enhances meaning and makes each thought system unique.

Thinking and learning are systemic processes. Just as facts were assumed to be the building blocks of knowledge, so thinking and learning were assumed to be inductive, linear processes. For example, a poster on the wall of a fifth grade classroom outlined the step-by-step approach that is ubiquitous in so-called "thinking skills" programs. A guide for teaching the thinking skill *synthesis,* the poster read as follows:

1. Delete trivial material.

2. Delete repetitious material.

3. Substitute a general term for a list of specific terms.

4. Combine a list of actions into a broad, single action.

5. Select a topic sentence.

6. Create a topic sentence.

In contrast, a deductive strategy for teaching a student how to synthesize a story might read: *Tell the story in one brief sentence.* The reader can decide which of these strategies is most natural and most effective.

While the inductive method — when used correctly — is appropriate to the empirically based scientific method, it is not an effective strategy for thinking/learning. As we have already seen, *the brain simply does not work that way!* Thinking and learning are systemic processes that *require a frame of reference for understanding and learning the parts.* This is true even with rote memory as evidenced by our propensity in preparation for examinations to create mnemonics as arbitrary frames of reference for organizing and remembering lists or groups of unrelated or uninteresting ideas. This tendency to create an arbitrary context is necessitated by the absence in most teaching of the use of "natural mnemonics," concepts such as Roszak's master ideas.

Humans are constructors of knowledge rather than discoverers of knowledge. Constructivism is a theory about the relationships between knowledge, learning, and meaning that draws on research in many fields, including cognitive psychology, physics, philosophy, and anthropology. "The theory defines knowledge as temporary, developmental, socially and culturally mediated, and thus, non-objective" (Brooks 1993). In short, "knowledge comes neither from the subject nor the object, but from the unity of the two." From this perspective, knowledge has more to do with *meaning and long-term understanding* than with formal descriptions of a "fixed world which the learner must come to know." According to the perspective of constructivism, each person is a constructor of knowledge and meaning.

While referring to the "structure of knowledge" can be misleading, it would be equally deceptive to suggest that knowledge is purely random.

There is no meaning without structure. What the constructivist theory suggests is that there is a significant correlation between the functional process I have called intelligence/thinking/learning and the way information and data are organized to create meaning. Educators Jacqueline and Martin Brooks (1993) highlight this correlation. "We learn by constructing new understandings of relationships and phenomena in our world ... not by discovering more, but interpreting through a different scheme or structure."

While constructivism is not a theory about teaching, it does suggest fundamental shifts in traditional classroom practices. If, as Brian Cambourne (1989) suggests, "The learner is the one who must make the connections, identify the patterns, and organize the bits," then it is incumbent upon educators to insure that both curriculum and instruction be organized in ways that enhance rather than discourage this kind of learning. To repeat the obvious, "learning how to learn" requires a radically different kind of education than is currently provided in most schools.

Curriculum must be organized systemically to reflect the natural process of intelligence/thinking/learning, to demonstrate the interrelationships among subjects, and to allow students to construct their own meaning. This book is about designing an integrated curriculum that is organized systemically. There is considerable confusion about what is meant by an integrated curriculum. For example, many educators will use the terms "integrated" and "interdisciplinary" interchangeably. This is unfortunate because these two approaches to curriculum design are as different as the ecological worldview and the technological worldview of Newtonian/Cartesian science. A truly integrated curriculum is organized to show "the connectedness of things," while an interdisciplinary curriculum is organized in ways that reinforce the separate and discrete character of academic disciplines. Recognizing that "the learner is the one who must make the connections, identify the patterns and organize the bits," the integrated curriculum is *preeminently learner-centered.* On the other hand, an interdisciplinary curriculum is content-centered — it begins with a given content that must be "learned." Although this content may be organized in a variety of different ways to demonstrate some of the connections among the various subjects (see Fogarty 1992; Jacobs 1989), it still reflects the traditional epistemological assumptions of Cartesian thought. While these organizational techniques may be helpful to the teacher who is seeking a how-to-manual, they do nothing to challenge the ruling mechanistic view of the world.

Thompson sixth grade team leader Ruth Ann Dunton reflects on her response to the integrated curriculum. "We began to see that integration is a way of thinking. There is no teachers' edition for it." She continues,

> [T]his freedom to be looking for connections is satisfying and fun. I am thinking about the world differently than I ever have. Maybe that is what was missing when I began my career. I can honestly say that the students are looking at the world differently, too. They are able to personalize their instruction as demonstrated in their written reflections throughout the year. Often their thoughts are a total surprise to me. They are comfortable with what they are doing and excited to share ideas…. I am comfortable with where I am and with the knowledge that I'll probably always be growing, changing, looking for answers, moving along in search of the big picture — just as I hope my students are.

Conclusion

Much of the resistance to an integrated, learner-centered curriculum is based on outdated assumptions about human nature and the innate capacities of children. Although we are reluctant to acknowledge it, for a very large number of children, schooling has been "basically negative, a progressive stripping away of dreams, an undermining of confidence" (Bateson 1994). While they may acquire skills and information, students are apt to learn more about limits to creativity than inherent human possibilities. For example, research (Howard 1980) shows that creativity scores invariably drop by 90% between the ages of five and seven. The downward trend continues so that by the time students reach age 40, most of them will have approximately 2% of the creativity they had as imaginative children.

But we don't need the research. I once watched my two-year-old granddaughter spend ten minutes trying to solve the problem of how to put on her diaper by herself. She laid it on the floor and tried lying on it. Then she tried sitting on it using a variety of postures. Next she carefully placed it in her rocking chair and tried to sit in it. She experimented with several other strategies, and although she never quite succeeded, she was not discouraged and would soon try again. Was she thinking or was she learning? The answer, of course, is YES to both questions!

Ask any parent who has tried to hide the cookie jar from a four-year-old about their problem-solving skills. Yet, by the time they reach third or fourth grade, we have to "teach" them problem-solving and other so-called thinking skills. And when they reach adolescence, we have convinced ourselves that they don't know enough to ask intelligent questions. What has happened to that innate capacity? The obvious reason, which many teachers are quick to acknowledge, is that, upon entering school, the child is programmed for fragmented, linear, sequential thinking that is antagonistic to the integrated, innate capacities for thinking and learning with which they are innately endowed.

I leave it to psychologist Charles Schmid (n.d.) to remind us of that which we intuitively know already.

> We're not really teaching anyone anything — we're unlocking what's already there, helping people get in touch with the enormous potential they already have, enabling them to regain that whole-brain balance they all had as imaginative children.

Chapter Three

Creating a
New Educational Vision

Until modern times young people could anticipate a future rather like that of their parents. Social change was that slow. Now young people face futures for which their parent's culture cannot prepare them. The young must create the future themselves. (Margaret Mead; emphasis added)

Before we can begin to design an integrated curriculum, we must define what is meant by curriculum. Most of us still think of *the curriculum* as content or subject matter — information that is the focus of classroom attention and what, presumably, students learn in school. Given this context, it logically follows that the only difference between the present, textbook-based curriculum and an integrated curriculum is the content/subject matter that is to be studied. Implicit in this view is the tacit assumption that if there is something wrong with the curriculum, it can be fixed in much the same way that a defective machine part can be fixed — by replacing the flawed part with a new one. Ideally, this would involve little more than purchasing a new set of integrated textbooks with different, integrated information in them. Nothing could be further from the reality.

Seventy-five years ago Alfred North Whitehead (1967) proposed that

"There is only one subject-matter for education, and that is Life in all its manifestations." Anthropologist Mary Catherine Bateson (1994) reinforces this point of view when she points out that the educational model created by our Western technological culture is the only one that defines curriculum in such a narrow way. "In other societies and times ... most of learning occurs outside the settings labeled as educational. Living and learning are everywhere founded on an improvisational basis." In their discussion of educational reform more than 15 years ago, Ernest Boyer and David Levine (n.d.) suggest that the curriculum focus on "the fundamental relationships, common experiences, and collective concerns that all humans share." Such a definition would include, as a minimum, *everything students experience/learn in school — by feeling, watching, thinking, and doing.* But even this definition is not broad enough to reflect "the fundamental relationships, common experiences, and collective concerns" of the real world. If we are to redefine *curriculum* as life in all its manifestations, we must also redefine the classroom to include the home, the community, and the world. In this expanded classroom everyone becomes both teacher and learner. Perhaps the *least* important component of this expanded educational experience is subject matter or content *as it is traditionally conceived.*

In order to reflect Life, an integrated curriculum must bridge the extensive network of chasms that exist among the various academic disciplines. Since the perspectives from which science, history or philosophy, mathematics, and art view life are obviously different, it should be equally obvious that these multiple viewpoints are complementary — no one of them can possess the ultimate or definitive perspective. Since the focus of each is the same, i.e., LIFE, it should also be obvious that there are extensive patterns of similarities and correlations among the many disparate academic subjects. Although it may be possible to catalog some of these similarities, the possible permutations are so numerous that no textbook could possibly accommodate them.

Our integrated curriculum must also bridge the chasm that currently exists between the classroom and the world beyond its doors. Since what lies beyond the doors in Los Angeles may have little in common with life in Evanston, Atlanta, Dallas, or Fort Dodge, any curriculum that reflects the interests, questions, and concerns of students must be situation-specific.

This means that *teachers must design their own integrated curricula.* But even that is no longer enough. If the curriculum is to be relevant to students in today's global information society, *students should be involved in the design process as much as possible.* In short, when designing a curriculum about life, there are no fixed rules and certainly no fixed content. There are, however, models, guidelines, and strategies like those presented in this book that may be used by teachers anywhere.

It is not necessary to start from scratch to design such a curriculum. Indeed, an integrated curriculum can even emerge within the constraints of traditional curriculum requirements. As seventh grade science teacher Bill O'Hagan discovered, it is possible to design a curriculum that meets all of the guidelines proposed here, while at the same time fulfilling departmental curriculum requirements. In this case, the departmental guidelines called for a unit on the human body. Bill began by asking students to identify the questions they wished to explore concerning the body. The results showed far more sophistication than he had anticipated from seventh grade students. Among some of the more obvious questions like "How do we hear?" "How do I speak?" and "How do I see?" were other more reflective questions: "What is puberty and why is it important?" "How are humans different from other animals?" "How do drugs affect the human body?" "What are the chances of getting skin cancer if I stay in, and stay out of the sun?" "How do organs work together?" "What happens when I am stressed?" "What do we really know about AIDS?" "How do I remember things?" "How do the cells in the body change?" Teams of students then decided on which questions they would research and present to the rest of the class. Integrated? Relevant? Provocative? Interesting? Substantive? The response of the students and the success of the unit was answer enough.

Barriers to an Integrated Curriculum

There are many barriers that keep teachers from embracing an integrated, learner-centered curriculum. My experience suggests that the major one may be fear of losing control of the classroom. Many teachers assume that a learner-centered classroom will lead to chaos. This is, of course, not true. Students recognize the necessity for structure and rules and when they "own" the rules, their will act responsibly. For example, students in one

second grade classroom established their own rules: 1) We work quietly —
library talk. 2) We share. 3) We put things back. 4) We plan our work and
ask our questions before the teacher starts an instructional group. Needless
to say, the rules worked.

A second barrier concerns motivation. The conventional wisdom
which says that children won't learn without some external reward or
punishment as a form of motivation is widespread among educators. It is
a great irony that in any discussion of motivation, the one factor that is
almost universally overlooked is student interest. Like the rest of us,
students learn what they are interested in learning! Every teacher has
experienced the "teachable moment" when a student's interest is suddenly
aroused by an "a ha!" event. Unfortunately, as teachers admit, such mo-
ments are rare. But they don't have to be. One creative and flexible kindergarten teacher designed an entire year's curriculum around a cocoon that
one of her students brought in the first week of school! Under her imaginative, inspired, and nurturing guidance, the kids kept making new connections, seeing new patterns and relationships, and expanding the scope of
their interests. She reports that the year was chock full of "a ha!" experiences
as kids explored their world with new eyes, new questions, and newly
acquired competencies. Like the rest of us, students don't want to spend
time learning what someone else thinks is important. If they are forced to,
unless we bribe them, they respond in the only way available to them —
they tune us out!

But resistance to a learner-centered curriculum goes beyond discipline, control, and motivation. Teachers who embrace the latest theories on
teaching and learning and are the first to implement new classroom methods like cooperative learning and portfolio assessments may still agree with
educators like E. D. Hirsh (1987), author of the *Cultural Literacy* curriculum
of core knowledge, that there is a basic set of concrete facts and hard data
— what Bateson calls the "hallowed certainties" — which children in
America need to learn in order to succeed in this society. This perspective
is reinforced by both district-and state-mandated curriculum guidelines
and by standardized testing programs that give priority to content-related
evaluations. These, of course, reflect a general cultural expectation evident
in the move to establish a national, content-based set of "world class"

standards for educational success. This perspective is perpetuated by the great majority of textbooks whose publishers are more concerned about presenting noncontroversial content in an attractive package than with relevance and substance. Unfortunately, since most adults today are products of an education based on such standards, it is difficult for them to appreciate their inherent fallacies.

There is still another concern — that students don't know enough to ask intelligent questions and certainly aren't ready to make decisions about their own learning. As one high school history teacher argued vehemently, "My students don't even know anything about world history. How can they ask intelligent questions about it?" There is also the tacit assumption that the only thing of interest to adolescent kids is learning how to get along with their peers in general, and the opposite sex in particular. While there is a great deal of truth in both observations, when students' interests are taken into consideration, such reservations are unjustified. Like Bill O'Hagan, Sharon Mulcahy decided to give students a chance to explore their own questions within the context of eighth grade departmental requirements, which called for a unit on light and sound. Admittedly with a high level of anxiety, Sharon asked her students what they wanted to know about light and sound. At the end of a month's investigation, students studied everything from lasers to the Hubble telescope — moving far beyond the scope of any eighth grade textbook. The unit had been the most successful, diverse, and sophisticated — and not so incidently the most enjoyable — she had ever conducted.

Finally, there is the assumption among some middle school teachers that many, if not most, of their students are still "concrete" learners who are not yet capable of the levels of abstraction called for by an integrated curriculum. However, even elementary teachers who have implemented the ideas discussed here have found — often contrary to their own expectations — that their students are almost uniformly capable of highly abstract and speculative thought. Because they have misunderstood Piaget's work, many teachers haven't recognized that *when learning is made relevant in "concrete" ways to their own experiences, students can make highly abstract associations and imaginative speculations* — in short, systems thinking.

Thompson teacher Ruth Ann Dunton describes the response of her sixth grade class to a systemic exploration of "culture."

> As students became familiar with terminology, they seemed able to make astounding connections. Their understandings of the workings of cultures seemed to be beyond their years. They were able to relate what they were discussing in class, regardless of time frame, to themselves. They took off on their own, finding answers to questions they wanted to answer. It was truly impressive. Learning seemed so natural, discussions were lively, reflections were personal yet worldly. Imagery writing done the first week of school and then at the end of the year on the same topic showed tremendous growth in concern and knowledge of their world.

Ironically, some of the more encouraging responses to this kind of curriculum have been from children with learning disabilities and behavioral disorders. One high school special education teacher reported that "acting out" virtually disappeared in the classes where she was implementing some of the strategies discussed here. Where special education students are included in regular, grade-level science and social studies classes, instead of their normal struggle to retain facts, these students do quite well when shown the "big picture" and how it relates to them.

Jean Humke, special education teacher at Thompson, has described how two of her students were able to participate fully in an eighth grade science class where the integrated content was far more sophisticated than would have been considered possible for them in previous years. Although one "bright" boy had good auditory and mechanical reasoning skills, he could not read a traditional science textbook. In lab and group project work, he became the leader in his group. Someone else did the reading and recording, and he took over the hands-on part. His motivation improved and disruptive classroom behaviors disappeared. Another of Jean's students — an eighth grade girl — at first wouldn't even answer questions in class. However, by the end of the semester she was making oral presentations on team projects right along with the other members of her team. One of the surprises was seeing how much the regular children benefitted from having the "specials" in the classroom.

Of all the barriers to substantive curriculum change, the most pernicious is the cynicism with which so many teachers have learned to live. It doesn't take long for a new, enthusiastic, visionary young woman or man to discover the political realities of institutional education. I have been confronted with this skepticism more times than I can remember from teachers who want to do things differently but whose hopes have been raised and dashed once too often. Because cynicism is difficult to express openly — especially to an administrator and sometimes even to oneself — teachers often raise the barriers discussed above as facades to protect themselves from the frustration, hurt, pain, and anger that many of them carry.

The point is that the barriers to an integrated curriculum, like most barriers to change, exist primarily, if not exclusively, in the mind. They reflect long-held, culturally conditioned assumptions that are not easy to relinquish — assumptions about schools and kids, about teaching and learning, and about life in general. Once these assumptions are identified and questioned, teachers are more willing to explore new ideas and risk new behaviors. Even then it is not easy. As eighth grade team leader Bonnie Pettebone observed, "These last three years have been the most difficult of my 19-year professional career. It's been like climbing out of a very deep hole." After a pause she added, " At the same time, they have been the most exhilarating and rewarding three years of my life." This kind of change is exceedingly difficult when faced alone. For most, it may be possible only with the support of a team of colleagues and the encouragement of an enthusiastic principal. This is why learning communities (See final chapter) are so necessary if substantive transformation is to occur in our schools.

An Integrated Curriculum Must Reflect a New Vision for Education

In a culture that actively fosters instant gratification, we seem to have forgotten the meaning and power of a long-term vision. In our frantic efforts to embrace the current fad, we are like the man who "jumped on his horse and rode off in all directions." In his conversation with Alice, the Cheshire Cat was more pragmatic. "If you don't know where you want to go, it doesn't matter which way you go from here." And so educators continue to promote whatever new program is in vogue, e.g., "multiple intelligences," "Outcome Based Education," or "TQM" (Total Quality Management), without any serious thought given to its long-term implications.

It seems to be a basic human need to have some sense of direction, a "vision of potential," for one's personal future. Children usually have some idea of what they want to be when they grow up; while their dreams may change as they approach adulthood, they will often spend many years and thousands of dollars in professional training in order to fulfill a personal vision. As might be expected, most of our personal visions are shaped by the dominant cultural norms of success reflected in the ubiquitous bumper sticker, "the one who dies with the most toys wins." Whatever vision exists also reflects the equally ubiquitous cultural norm of progress — the incremental expansion of human potential — engineered by technology — "ever upward" toward some undefined infinite horizon. In spite of the "downturns" in the economy, foreign competition, political chicanery and gridlock, and even holes in the ozone layer, most Americans seem to have an almost childlike faith that the *long-term future* is going to be a continuation of the present — only better. Only recently has this vision begun to be suspect. Unfortunately, few of us have an alternative vision to replace the one we have tacitly accepted.

Although most of us take our personal life-goals for granted, we are oblivious of the degree to which such cultural visions shape institutional behavior. For example, as long as the dominant cultural vision is that the next 25 years will be essentially an accelerated version of the past and present, educational policy and practice will continue in its present form. While a few new programs will be introduced, nothing essential will change. As teachers become increasingly cynical, their cynicism will be tempered by the never-ending seductive promises of powerful new technologies designed to make their jobs easier by transforming teaching and learning. According to this scenario, educational reform will consist of an endless series of innovative, patchwork programs, each of which has its "day in the sun" and then quietly fades into oblivion. Instead of embracing nicely packaged programs, we should be embracing visions.

If educational transformation is to become a reality, we must create a vision of education that is powerful enough to call forth the passion, energy, and untapped potential necessary to bring it into being. Peter Senge of MIT's Sloan School of Management has found that the level of commitment required to bring about *any* substantive organizational transformation requires a long-term perspective that is inspired by a powerful vision. "People do not focus on the long term because they *have* to, but because they *want* to. In every instance where one finds a long-term view actually operating in human affairs, there is a long-term vision at work" (Senge 1990).

A generation ago John Kennedy created a national long-term vision of placing a man on the moon. Based on certain untested assumptions about our scientific and technological potential, this evocative vision literally transformed that potential into a reality. It wasn't long before the impact of Kennedy's long-term vision was felt in schools throughout America as science and math programs were strengthened and, in time, transformed.

The challenge to our generation is to create a cultural vision of a possible future for the next century that can capture our collective imaginations in the same way that Kennedy's vision did a generation ago. To paraphrase Daniel Burnam, chief architect of the 1893 Columbian Exhibition in Chicago and author of the first master plan for that city — no small dreamer himself — "Have no little visions. They have no magic to stir men's blood!"

In the absence of a coherent cultural vision that challenges the status quo, it will not be easy for educators to evoke a vision of potential compelling enough to transform educational policy and practice. For some, the possibilities of liberating the unrealized potential of their students is challenge enough. For others, the challenges presented by a learner-centered, integrated curriculum will energize them because it taps into their own imaginative idealism. For the majority who have seen too many programs come and go, these challenges alone are not sufficient to cut through their passivity. Although a few schools and classrooms will be transformed, education as a whole will continue relatively unaffected. The only thing that will overcome the cynicism and apathy and lead to systemic transformation is a vision of potential that will challenge the imaginations of educators in the same way Kennedy's vision challenged an entire nation. Since no such vision seems to be forthcoming in the political arena, enlightened teachers may have to create their own vision of the future.

It is appropriate that the space program — probably the greatest scientific and technological achievement of the twentieth century — provides us with the perspective necessary for such a vision. In a recent interview, America's senior astronaut, F. Story Musgrave (1994), described his space walk to repair the Hubble Space Telescope.

> The view of Earth — as something whole and interconnected — may be the most important thing to come out of the space program. That and a new sense of oneself as a 'planetary citizen' — a citizen of the globe…. You have that big picture which can be really magical, of the entire forest as opposed to just seeing one tree at a time.

Given the twin realities that, like it or not, we are "planetary citizens" who face a set of ubiquitous global dilemmas, I suggest that the only vision that is powerful enough to reshape our educational system is a vision in which the present generation of students are *planetary citizens living cooperatively at peace in the global village*. Just as Kennedy's grand vision transformed science and math education, so a vision of global cooperation, because of its profound relevance to every facet of life, can transform the entire educational system. The relevance of this "macro" vision to educational transformation lies in the fact that it resonates at many different levels with the "micro" visions held by many teachers. For one thing, it reflects the cooperative learning and community building experiences that are beginning to make a real difference in many schools.

Even more significantly, a vision of cooperative behavior often touches teachers at a deep personal level because it reflects the dreams and aspirations that inspired them to enter the profession. Time after time over a 20-year period, I have asked teachers in my workshops to share the vision that motivated them to become teachers. When they begin to describe what their ideal or dream classroom would look like if they could teach the way they always wanted to, invariably they envision a classroom and curriculum similar to that discussed here. They have no difficulty imagining kids freely and cooperatively pursuing ideas, activities, projects, and questions of genuine interest to them.

Finally, a vision of global cooperation triggers a hope that lies deep within the human psyche — to live in a peaceful world in which everyone has enough and people can be free to pursue their own interests. While most teachers suspect that global cooperation is little more than a fantasy, they are willing to embrace it because they see the obvious correlation between the attitudes and behaviors being learned in cooperative classrooms and those necessary to make global cooperation a reality. In the absence of a cultural vision of this magnitude, the schools may be the best place to plant the seeds for a vision of global cooperation. Because children are by nature optimistic and because it is *their* future we are talking about, at least we can make certain they gain the knowledge and competencies necessary for participation and success in a global information society. In addition, it just may be that by prefiguring global cooperation in thousands of classrooms across our country, we are nurturing a vision of a possible future that will capture their imagination and energize them toward that end.

Since people only pursue long-term visions *because they want to* — I suggest that the first step in educational reform should be to invite teachers to "think big" and *create a vision of the future they desire.* In situations where teachers have been encouraged by superintendents or principals to create visions that reflect their deepest aspirations and dreams, they respond with the enthusiasm, passion, and commitment that can turn their dreams into reality precisely because they want to do it. Indeed, my informal surveys suggest that in many cases teachers would prefer having the freedom and support necessary to create their own ideal classrooms and schools than receive annual salary increments.

A Vision Must Relate to the Real World

While it is necessary that a vision for education reflect the dreams of teachers, it must also reflect the real world. Otherwise, it will be little more than fantasy. But educators cannot continue to think like the generals who, it is said, are always preparing for the last war. Because, as Margaret Mead observed, "young people face futures for which their parent's culture cannot prepare them," we cannot base a long-term vision on present, short-term realities. The world of 2020 A.D., when today's students achieve positions of responsible leadership, will not look like today's world. In order to prepare these students to *create the future themselves*, we must exercise what James Botkin (1979) calls "anticipatory thinking" or what I call "systems thinking." Unless we can anticipate what life may be like in the early decades of the next century, we cannot identify the kinds of knowledge and competencies that students will require to fully and creatively participate in the decisions that shape their lives. There are three arenas in which students must be prepared to participate. The first and most immediate is the marketplace.

Any discussion about education for life in the twenty-first century must begin with what is euphemistically called economic necessity. Students must acquire the knowledge and competencies to successfully compete in the marketplace — a marketplace that has been literally transformed over the past century. Until World War II, the marketplace for most Americans was local. People found jobs where they lived. In part due to the Great Depression, but primarily because of wartime demands, the marketplace became national with more and more people moving to where the jobs were. Today the marketplace is global. And while most Americans will never actually work overseas, the global nature of the marketplace will shape the economy of every nation in the world in ways that as yet cannot be fully anticipated.

Robert Reich (1992) is probably correct when he identifies the symbolic analyst as the prototypical occupation for which many of the brightest and the best will compete. These will be the professional managers and technicians whose job will be "to identify, solve, and broker problems" that may arise anywhere in the world. Although Reich's implicit assumption is that there will be enough of these jobs for everyone who wants one, this clearly will not be the case. Since the majority of students will have neither the capability nor the inclination to become symbolic analysts, they will look for well-paying jobs in the more traditional occupations. However, if projections are correct, these are often the very jobs that are being eliminated by downsizing or replaced by automation. Given such limitations, the successful will be those who are skilled at what Mary Catherine Bateson (1994) calls "learning along the way." They will have the ability to master new competencies quickly and adapt previously learned ones to new and often diverse circumstances. Many others will become self-employed entrepreneurs. A decade ago Peter Drucker (1985), probably America's foremost management authority, noted the emergence of a new entrepreneurial economy that was even then transforming American business, the American workforce, and American society. He predicted that this "middle tech" and "low tech" economy, based on "systemic innovation, entrepreneurial management, and entrepreneurial strategies," will continue to shape major sectors of the national economy in the foreseeable future. Ten years later, as the accuracy of his predictions suggests, it is possible to project an even greater impact of entrepreneurial activity on both the national but global marketplace in the decades to come. In order to be prepared for such a role — and who at 18 or 22 knows if they will someday work for themselves — functional literacy for potential entrepreneurs will include those skills necessary to be self-directed and work well alone or with others. These are, of course, the proficiencies that are essential for learning how to learn.

The second arena in which today's students must be prepared to actively participate is the social/political. Just as economic necessity dictates that people work for their living, social necessity dictates that in a democracy unless they are willing to allow others to make decisions for them, people must participate responsibly in the decisions that shape their lives. Observing the increased apathy of the American electorate, the late historian Christopher Lasch (1995) argued that the greatest threat to democracy will come, not from military dictatorships, but rather from the new, elite class of scientific managers of whom Reich's symbolic analyst is the prototype. Already, in the face of massive apathy and inertia, *by default* these professional managers and technicians are already making the political, economic, social, and environmental decisions that are shaping life in the global village — decisions that nations will not or cannot make for themselves. Lasch writes,

> Today it is the elites — those who control the international flow of money and information, preside over philanthropic foundations and institutions of higher learning, manage the instruments of cultural production and thus set the terms of public debate — who ... abandon the middle class, divide the nation, and betray the idea of a democracy for all America's citizens.

He argues that the only viable alternative to some form of benign global oligarchy is one Thomas Jefferson proposed two centuries ago

> I know of no safe depository of the ultimate power of the society but the people themselves; and if we think them not enlightened enough to exercise their control with a wholesome discretion, *the remedy is not to take it from them but to inform their discretion.* (emphasis added)

While thoughtful people may disagree about the extent of the danger facing democratic institutions, I think we would all agree that education for the twenty-first century must prepare students to embrace both the privileges and responsibilities of citizenship in order to participate fully and thoughtfully in the decisions that will shape their lives.

The rationale for a third arena of participation has already been established in the discussion above. Whether our children like it or not, they will be planetary citizens. Whether they are prepared or not, they will inherit a set of profound and seemingly intractable global dilemmas that, if allowed to continue unresolved, may destroy civilization as we know it. If they are not prepared to exercise the privileges and responsibilities of planetary citizenship, there already exists an elite class of technocrats prepared to address the multiple crises that will become full-blown in the next decade. The only alternative may well be some form of global cooperation based on democratic principles of self-governance. To accomplish this goal will require a fundamentally different way of thinking about ourselves and our relationship to the world — a way of thinking psychologist Roger Walsh calls a "global psychology" — the ability to think globally and act locally. Without negating the necessity for effective scientific management at both national and global levels, I am suggesting that *unless scientific management in all its myriad forms is shaped and driven by a powerful vision of an egalitarian form of global cooperation based on democratic principles of self-governance,* it will become a tool of absolute control by an elite class of technocrats whose benign vision of "one world" is a global village held together by military and technological might — Orwell's *1984* twenty-five years later. To counter this, today's students must be prepared as adults to assume both the privileges and the responsibilities of global citizenship.

In light of these real-world necessities, our educational vision/mission must be one in which *teachers and students are working cooperatively to insure that every student who graduates is functionally literate, that is, they are prepared to respond deliberately and creatively to the demands of economic necessity, enlightened and informed social responsibility, and qualified planetary citizenship.*

In a generalized way, functional literacy includes flexibility, transferability of skills, proficiency in anticipating problems, an aptitude for knowing more with less information, the capacity to improvise by making decisions without enough information, a willingness to do more and be

satisfied with less, tolerance for and the ability to work and live cooperatively in the midst of diversity, change, ambiguity, uncertainty, and paradox,
a high level of self-direction and personal discipline, and skill in listening
carefully, articulating clearly, and resolving conflicts peacefully. Finally,
functional literacy must include the capacity to consciously and deliberately create personal and collective visions of desired futures and the
competencies necessary to make those futures manifest. This is a tall order.
But I would argue that functional literacy is, and always has been, the
essentially innate capacity that has enabled humans to not only survive but
thrive. If functional literacy is a desired outcome for our graduates, teachers
must find ways to tap their own and their students' innate capacities, thus
enabling students to acquire the intrinsically different and distinctive types
of insight, knowledge, and skill competencies discussed below.

The Insights, Knowledge, and Skills Required for Functional Literacy

The primary insight for calling forth this innate potential is the intuitive
understanding that we live in a universe where everything is connected to
everything else. Fundamental to a global psychology, this insight is also the
indispensable source and essence of personal empowerment. If everything
is connected to everything else, then each individual makes a difference
because everything one does affects everything else. While for most of us
this understanding will begin as an espoused theory, once it is transformed
into a theory-in-use, thinking and acting in terms of connectedness will
become second nature.

The core of common knowledge that unlocks our innate knowing is *an
intrinsically different kind of knowledge* than the fact-based knowledge that
has dominated education since its beginning. In a society "drowning in
information and starved for knowledge," an educational system that
stresses the *quantity* of information over the *quality* of information is woe-
fully out of touch with reality.

The kind of knowledge necessary to become a lifelong learner is the
kind that enables one to know more with less information. To return to Story
Musgrave's analogy, while in the past education has focused on the trees,

it must now focus on the "big picture … of the entire forest as opposed to just seeing one tree at a time." This "big picture" knowledge highlights the whole rather than the parts. Like the picture of a jigsaw puzzle, it provides a context for understanding the structure and the relationships that enables one to see how the puzzle pieces fit together.

Every academic discipline is in essence a thought system with its own internal structure or conceptual framework. This structure consists of the concepts and principles that are essential to the discipline and the way it is organized. Once you have grasped this structure (the big picture), it is relatively simple to identify the specific relationships and detailed information that you wish to investigate or is relevant to your need. In short, with this systems perspective, *you know how to learn what you need to learn, when you need to learn it.*

This common core includes the knowledge of whole systems, knowledge of the principles that govern all living systems, intuitive knowledge, and contextual knowledge.

Knowledge of whole systems. Our understanding of how living systems work as undifferentiated wholes is based on studies in ecology. Because the planetary ecological systems are the most basic systems on Earth, they are the prototype for all systems. Indeed, a case can be made that all living systems are intrinsically ecological systems.

Knowledge of the fundamental principles and concepts that govern all living systems. These principles and concepts provide the conceptual framework for understanding the connectedness of things. Because of their universal applicability to all thought systems, they are powerful cognitive bridges that make possible the transfer of learning from one arena to another.

Intuitive knowledge. Intuition is our way of tapping into the genetic knowledge and archetypal wisdom that characterize the human species. This capacity for direct knowledge of the world is the source of imagination, ingenuity, and creativity.

Contextual knowledge. This is the kind of knowledge that emerges from what Mary Catherine Bateson (1994) calls "peripheral vision" — the ability to recognize patterns and relationships. This knowledge of connections and correlations is the kind of knowledge that enables one to explore, understand, and create contexts of meaning.

The skill competencies necessary to become a lifelong learner are embedded in and activated by the integrative process I call systemic thinking/learning. These include competence in what are often referred to as the basics, self-reflection, communication and dialogue, and living responsibly.

The so-called basics: Reading, writing, math, and computer literacy. Contrary to conventional wisdom, both research and experience make it clear that success in the so-called basics is contingent upon having a "big picture" perspective. Just as children learn language and numbers experientially and contextually, when given an appropriate conceptual framework, people can readily master the details of reading, writing, and mathematics.

Self-reflective consciousness: Thinking about the way we think, the way we make decisions, and reflecting on the consequences of those decisions. Our ability to make conscious or thoughtful — full of thought — decisions is contingent upon the capacity to reflect upon our thought processes, feelings, and actions. Self-reflection includes the capacity for unbiased self-assessment and is essential to critical and creative thinking, indeed, to all of the so-called higher order thinking strategies. In addition, self-reflective consciousness includes the capacity for disciplined contemplation, visualization, and imagination.

The fundamental human capacities for communication and dialogue, cooperation, conflict resolution, empathy, and artistic self-expression, e.g., through art, music, dance, drama, and storytelling. Humans are by nature social animals with the innate capacities necessary to live harmoniously in close association with other humans. These human potentials can only fully emerge when one is an integral part of a community of learners. Here one can learn to listen with open ears and see with open eyes. Here one can experience empathy. Only in community can one learn to speak directly, without dissemblance or ambiguity. When we are members of a learning community, we are free to express ourselves in whatever modes we choose, knowing that the community is enriched by our presence.

The capacity to live responsibly. Responsibility comes from a Latin root word meaning "to pledge or promise." This means that responsibility is a way of living in relationship. Responsibility is grounded in what might be called emotional literacy or personal integrity, that is, the integration of all of our relationships — to ourselves, to others, and to the great mystery of life.

Genuine responsibility can only be learned when one is free to make mistakes. Thus, it has little meaning apart from a community of learners where mistakes are understood to be integral to the learning process. Here, one learns to be accountable for one's own feelings, beliefs, values, learnings, decisions, and life choices. Here one can fully accept, honor, and celebrate one's humanness with all of its paradoxes, ambiguities, uncertainties, and inconsistencies. Because responsibility can be learned and expressed only in community, its ultimate expression is learning to live with and do for others as we would have them live with and do for us — the Golden Rule. In essence, to live responsibly means living a life of service to fellow humans and to all living things.

All of the above might be summarized in two well-known injunctions: "Know thyself" and "To thine own self be true." While at first glance the list of knowledge and competencies may appear idealistic, they have been part of the lives of women and men throughout history and are evident in the experience of humans in every culture from prehistory to the present. They describe what Jean Houston calls "the possible human" and represent the *sine qua non* for our children and succeeding generations.

Whether they are prepared to do so or not, our children will create their own future. Their choices may well be between global cooperation or interminable armed conflict; between living productively in a world that honors human rights and community values or existing marginally in a world filled with greed, anger, crime, violence, and fear; between accepting the necessity to share scarce resources so that everyone has enough or facing the inevitable destiny of ecological catastrophe. Given these alternatives, every thoughtful person would choose the former. Just as future choices will be made by our children and their children, at this juncture in human history, the choice is ours to make. Although we prefer to deny it, to a significant extent *our children's future will depend on the future that we choose.* The great educational challenge is to adequately prepare the present generation of children to make wise decisions about their future.

Conclusion

Many men on the Western frontier taught themselves to read and write. Carrying dog-eared copies of the Bible, Blackstone, Dickens, and other nineteenth century classics, they learned to read by firelight and pondered what they had read as they rode herd in the stillness of the night. A few, without the help of any formal schooling, became competent teachers, ministers, lawyers, and politicians. This leads one to wonder how they were able to do this without the aid of teachers, textbooks, phonics, worksheets, or a grading system. It also raises the question of why people today can't seem to learn as naturally as men and women did a century ago before modern schools were invented.

I believe the answer is succinctly stated in the words of my middle son who on the night before he began school said to his mother, "You know mom, today was the last day of my life that I could do what I want to do when I want to do it." And so he went off to be educated — to be socialized — to be enculturated — to learn to be a productive citizen. And what did he learn? He learned that knowledge was clearly divided into neatly labeled little boxes like science and math and history. He learned that life was ruled by clocks and bells. He learned that the rewards came when you listened to the teacher and memorized what she told him was important. He learned to raise his hand to ask questions, and that some questions — like "What is life all about?" aren't good questions to ask in school. He learned to tune out when things got tough.

And while, in spite of the system, my son "made it," many don't. And, ironically, the price of failure is paid not only by those who didn't make it, but also by our society that — believe it or not — seems bent on stamping out most of that enormous energy, curiosity, potential, and creativity that is the heritage and birthright of all children. The time has come to transform the educational system so that this generation of children and the next and the next are truly empowered to embrace an educational perspective that is contextual and to create a better and more humane world for themselves and for humankind.

Chapter Four

Creating a Context for Teaching and Learning

> Events do not happen in a vacuum, but in a social, political, cultural, and economic context.... The important thing is to craft your own worldview [as a context] ... to guide your work, ideas, relationship and contributions to society. (*Megatrends 2000*)

One of the most disastrous consequences of our almost total reliance on fragmented thinking is the tendency to ignore context. As I pointed out in Chapter Two, the analytical methodology of science breaks complex wholes into simple, discrete component parts. It then proceeds to study and *assign a precise meaning to,* i.e., define, each part. Implicit in this methodology is the assumption that *meaning is inherent in the self-evident parts that can be encapsulated in the assigned definition.* A tree is a tree is a tree, and a maple tree is always and only a maple tree. By definition, a tree can be nothing other than tree. With the introduction of the scientific/technological system of belief, definitions became increasingly important and, in time, have come to dominate not only our understanding of things but also our perception of things. Like blind men exploring an elephant, we tend to see things in terms of their defined qualities — as separate, discrete entities, complete in and of themselves. Wholes are perceived as being nothing more than a collection of individual parts. A forest is nothing more than an aggregate of individual trees that happen to be growing in proximity. Implicit in this perspective is the assumption that *the whole is equal to a sum of its parts.* Larger meanings can be discovered only by first understanding the parts and then incrementally reconstructing the whole.

And so teachers continue to present facts as isolated building blocks of knowledge and treat each academic discipline as though it were a discrete body of knowledge. One high school student wryly summarized the present curriculum.

> English is not history and history is not science and science is not art and art is not music. Art and music are minor subjects and English and history and science are major subjects. A subject is something you "take." When you have "taken" it, you have "had" it, and when you have "had" it, you are immune and need not take it again. (Postman and Weingartner 1969)

In science students still learn the scientific method as an "objective" methodology that can be used to solve problems by isolating the variable. This strategy is much like isolating a single frame of a motion picture and assuming that you understand the plot of the film and can solve the mystery from it. In short, virtually the entire teaching/learning process to which students are exposed reinforces the illusions of separateness and objectivity. As a result, students soon begin to believe that the world really is this way.

On the other hand, systems thinking recognizes that *because the whole is greater than the sum of its parts, no single, discrete entity can be fully understood apart from the complex whole of which it is an integral part.* The whole provides the context without which our knowledge of the part is necessarily limited. To return to our example of the tree and the forest, while a tree can be described with detailed precision, our understanding of a tree will always be limited until we can study it in the context of its habitat, the forest or meadow ecosystem to which it belongs. In short, *systems thinking is contextual thinking.* It recognizes that without a context, meaning is truncated and incomplete.

Creating Contexts of Meaning

Futurist Willis Harman (1988) defines *context* as *the meaning connection.* To design a curriculum is to create "contexts of meaning." Because most textbook authors, curriculum committee members, and teachers don't think contextually, the context they create is unpremeditated and almost accidental. The result is most often a curriculum that is, to use Leslie Hart's phrase, "brain antagonistic." Thus, it is important for the teacher who is designing an integrated curriculum to understand what it means to create contexts of meaning.

To do this, it is first necessary to recognize the significance of context in our daily lives. Although we seldom think about it, events never occur in a vacuum but in a cultural context consisting of a complex network of social, economic, political, and ecological influences and relationships. It is these relationships and not the events themselves that enable us to make meaning out of our experiences. In the words of Thompson team leader Chuck Robinson, "The context is what is becoming most important and kids then have ownership. They no longer ask 'Why do we do this'?"

Although we may be unaware of it, we are constantly receiving contextual feedback, i.e., information, vis-à-vis these relationships. Again, whether we are aware of it or not, this information both *informs and forms us* (Wheatley 1992). *This information is the context* that frames and thus provides meaning to the daily events of our lives. Although we are seldom aware of it, we are intuitively scanning this context as we continually monitor it for meaning.

The pragmatic quality of context is reflected in the experience of Thompson math teacher Mary Pat Ryan. Her team leader, Lin Stacey, was introducing his seventh grade science class to the use of data. He explained to his students that one way to display the data was by using a circle graph or pie chart. Mary Pat immediately recognized a teachable moment for introducing students to the concept of a circle. Her voice rang with enthusiasm as she shared this experience with her colleagues.

> It took me no more than 10 minutes to have everyone in class understand the idea of multiplying the percentage times 360 degrees. In other years I would spend two or three days on that topic and then be frustrated at how many students still did not understand the concept. Here, in less than a class period, everyone knew and could use the knowledge. Why? Because it was important and meaningful to them. They had a context for learning.

To create a context means that, either deliberately or inadvertently, we take something out of its given context, in this case, a textbook example, and replace it with our own context of meaning. In so doing, we literally change the meaning. Rather than accepting someone else's interpretation that is implicit in the original context, we provide our own interpretation of events.

This is particularly relevant to our modern society where — to use John Naisbitt's mixed metaphors — we are "drowning in information and starved for knowledge." Because of information overload — much of it sterile trivia — it is perplexingly difficult to try to interpret for oneself the vast amounts of data that inundate us. Given our extraordinarily busy lives, it is seductively simple and far less complicated to accept the interpretation of events — the "spin" — created by those who make and report the "news." By controlling not only what we are allowed to hear — which may include deliberate disinformation, e.g., the 1991 Gulf War (PBS, Frontline, January 9, 1996) and the 1994 Health Care Plan (Carlson and Hey 1994) — but how it is interpreted, those in power (the ubiquitous *they*) promulgate *their* "contexts of meaning." This is the way thought control works. By shaping the way we think *they* are able to manipulate our decisions.

Recognizing the danger of this kind of thought control, John Naisbitt advises that "the important thing is to craft your own [context] to guide your work, ideas, relationships, and contributions to society." He warns,

> Without some context as a frame of reference you won't know what to look for; what information will be most useful to you; what information will answer *your* questions. As a result, not only will the vast amount of data that comes your way each day whiz by you, but you will spend your time answering *their* questions and thinking the way *they* want you to think. (Naisbitt and Aburdene 1990)

In short, unless you have your own clearly defined frame of reference you won't know whether everything is relevant or whether, as Joseph Heller's more mature Yossarian observes, "Nothing makes sense and neither did everything else."

Kurt Anderson addresses the increasing significance of context at Thompson.

> The principle of *context* has truly been the driving force of change in our building. Understanding that when there is no context, there is no meaning, has caused faculty members in and across teams to question all that they do. Consequently, what used to be a traditional study of Europe in

Dan Kroll's seventh grade geography class has been transformed into a multi-disciplinary, collaborative investigation of the question, "Why can't the European nations become the United States of Europe?"

Four Contextual Relationships

There are four fundamental relationships that shape any given situation. These four relationships are fundamental in two ways. First, they are global in that they incorporate all other relationships. Second, they are ubiquitous so that to overlook any one of them is to neglect a significant and relevant facet of the situation.

There four relationships are:

- *The Subjective Context: Our relationship to ourselves and others.* Here we recognize and express the subjective and participatory nature of knowledge, experience, and reality.

- *The Time Context: Our relationship to the past, present, and future.* Here we recognize and learn from the historical, developmental, and evolutionary perspectives.

- *The Symbolic Context: Our relationship to the world of information and knowledge.* Here we recognize the significance of ideas, symbols, and metaphors in shaping our thoughts and actions.

- *The Ecosystem or Global Context: Our relationship to the physical world.* Here we consider our experiences of physical reality, the biosphere, and the global ecological systems.

If teachers — and hopefully, students — are to consciously and deliberately create contexts of meaning, it is important to understand the nature of these four relationships and how they influence the ways we think and live in the world.

The Subjective Context

The focus of the *Subjective Context* is on two relationships — our relationship with ourselves and our relationship with others. To begin with, we must recognize that all of our perceptions of the world are filtered through subjective lenses — our preconceived maps of reality. Our minds literally won't let us see what doesn't fit these mental maps. While some people may wear rose-colored glasses, our lenses come in as many diverse hues as there are people. Although the illusion of objectivity — that there is one "right" way to see things — is deeply embedded in our thinking, we must remember that while it may be useful at times, it is an illusion. Because of these subjective mental models of the world, in a very significant way, we create our own reality — a reality that is expressed through our opinions, biases, prejudices, values, and most importantly obviously, through our actions. We can no more shed our subjective perspectives than we can shed our skins. What we can do is to identify them, lay them on the table, acknowledge their influence, and then hold them as tentative pending new insights, knowledge, and information. Because our mental models reflect certain basic assumptions about how the world works — assumptions that for the most part are culturally ordained — they can be examined and, if one so chooses, replaced with other assumptions that more nearly reflect personal choice.

One has only to study the pattern of family relationships in diverse cultures to recognize that *our relationship to other people* is also culturally ordained. For example, the nuclear family is a recent Western cultural construct. So, too, is the assumption that the good of the individual is the highest good and the "common good" is contingent upon satisfying competing, individual self-interests. Any study of comparative cultures makes it clear that whether one is predominately competitive or cooperative is more a matter of cultural inheritance than genetic DNA. This means, of course, that we have a choice as to how we live in relationship with others. I believe the time has come to acknowledge that because humans are fundamentally social creatures, community, not the individual, is the basic ontological unit of human society. Since we are rational beings who can make conscious choices, it may be time for to relearn the rules and skills of living in community. The first and most pragmatic rule of community living is familiar to us all — we call it the Golden Rule — treat others the same way we want to be treated. What is left unsaid is that when we live this way, we find that others are willing to live this way as well.

Chuck Robinson's eighth grade team at Thompson decided to have the students spend a week exploring "Who am I?" The concluding activity was to be a series of cardboard sculptures illustrated by personal memorabilia, e.g., pictures, banners, toys, and other objects that reflected facets of one's "self." To demonstrate the activities, the teachers prepared their own sculpture and presented it to the entire team of 125 students. The experience was a deeply moving one as teachers used many personal items and shared personal experiences that, just a year ago, they never would have considered. As a result, students followed suit. In Chuck's words, "Boys shared teddy bears and girls shared dolls." In short, the activity became a powerful experience in team sharing and bonding that included not only students but teachers as well.

Thompson's Jan Sutfin also provides us with another example of how subjective issues find their way into a learner-centered curriculum.

> The issue of prejudice became the focal point during the winter. In trying to define or put meaning to the word, one student stated that she "was prejudiced against popular kids." I used this as an opening to expand the context of a single student's experience by asking if others ever felt this way. Soon others shared their prejudices, some of them even acknowledged that they had prejudice against themselves. Soon the students, without further guidance from me, began to recognize how jealousy, envy, fear and hate were related to their feelings of prejudice. By the end of the discussion, everyone agreed that the root cause of prejudice was fear. By this time it was clear that all of the students had a real understanding of prejudice and its implications in our culture.
>
> The next day one of the students came into class and said, "Mrs. Sutfin, I had the neatest thing happen yesterday. My friend and I talked about God and whether God was black or white or man or woman. And what it would be like and if it made any difference. It was a real neat talk. We never talked that way before. It was really neat."

Jan concludes, "Trust these kids. They are capable of a lot more than we have given them credit for in the past."

To summarize, "In the subjective context we recognize the subjective nature of human knowledge and experience, focus on individual responsibility, explore the value implications when making decisions, and emphasize the individual in community" (Goetz and Janz 1987).

The Time Context

The focus of the *Time Context* is on our relationship to the past and to the future and how we integrate these two perspectives into our personal and collective present. Conventional wisdom has always drawn heavily on the past — traditions, historical precedents, personal experience — for guidance in present decisions. While we tacitly acknowledge the presence of some future possibility, for the most part, our views of the future are shaped by the past. As I have already suggested, the tendency to see the future in terms of the past is particularly troublesome when it comes to our collective future. Thus, we assume that problems like poverty and war are part of the inevitable nature of things. While there is much to learn from the past, when it becomes the primary criterion for action, we are doomed to repeat it.

Jean Houston points out that ours is the first generation in history with the benefit of the full sweep of human experience — from the earliest human almost three million years in the past to the furthest scope of human imagination — Issac Assimov's Galactic Empire perhaps 20,000 years in the future. Given this evolutionary perspective, Marilyn Ferguson reminds us that "our past is not our potential.... Where we are going is more important than where we have come from." In short, the time has arrived when the future must become the primary context for making the decisions that will shape not only our lives but our children's lives to the seventh generation. It is with this perspective in mind that professionals in the field of organizational transformation (Senge 1990; Wheatley 1992; Hawken 1994; Korten 1995) place so much emphasis on the role of vision in organizational and social transformation.

During the annual residential outdoor education program at George Williams College on Lake Geneva, Wisconsin, Thompson sixth graders had an opportunity to expand their understanding of the Time Context by interviewing members of an Elderhostel program. Immediate feedback from both the students and the Elderhostelers alike made it clear that for everyone this cross-generational experience had been a huge success. Students heard firsthand what it was like to live through different times, e.g., during the Great Depression, and to grow up in different circumstances, e.g., on a farm. In teams, students were later able to explore and share their experiences by creating a book telling the tales they had heard through poetry, stories, cartoons, advertisements, flip books, and other inventive illustrations. One team even made a doll depicting their senior friend and videotaped their re-creations of the stories that they had heard. This two-month *contextual process* culminated with the mailing of copies of the book (including a photograph of each interview taking place) to the Elderhostelers.

To summarize, "In the Time Context we explore our relationship to time and change, incorporate an evolutionary perspective on time and change, and incorporate the historical perspective and the future perspective" (Goetz and Janz 1987).

The Symbolic Context

The focus of the *Symbolic Context* has several dimensions. This is the arena of human thought where we explore the ideas, knowledge, and symbols that *inform and thus form us*, making it possible for us to understand the world and communicate with each other. Here we become aware of the degree to which *language as symbol* creates and configures both what we think and the way we think — which in turn prefigures and thus shapes our actions. Because of the precision of our language, patterned as it has been by the scientific perspective, we have a tendency to mistake our symbols for the reality that they represent. Ken Wilber (1981) explains our dilemma:

> Our problem is that we create a conventional map, complete with boundaries, of the actual territory of nature which has no boundaries, and then thoroughly confuse the two. As Korzybski and the general semanticists have pointed out, our words, symbols, signs, thoughts and ideas are merely maps of reality, not reality itself, because "the map is not the territory." The word "water" won't satisfy your thirst. While it is fine to map out the territory, it is fatal to confuse the two.

Language not only reveals what we think, it shapes the way we think as well. For example, I used to believe that becoming fluent in a new language was only a matter of substituting unfamiliar grammar and syntax for the familiar grammar and syntax of my own language — essentially a word-for-word correlation. I now realize that people who speak different languages think differently so that learning grammar and syntax is only the first step toward fluency. For example, when I was conducting a workshop in Mexico I found that Mexicans seldom ask direct questions. They seemed to wander around and finally came in through the back door so subtly that I often wasn't sure whether the question had been asked and if so, what it was. I soon learned that, for them, the way to ask a question is to first create a context for the question. I began to suspect that English — where definitions are precise and distinct — may be the only language that is not implicitly contextual. For example, Chinese and Japanese are highly contextual languages — the context is implicit in the visual images projected by the ideograms. In Navajo and other Native American languages, distinctions that are so important to us — such as those between "mind" and "body" — do not exist. As a result of these differences, Native Americans think differently than Anglos — a source of much misunderstanding, confusion, and suffering.

Finally, the Symbolic Context, which I used to call the Information Context, focuses our attention on the way we use information, the amount of information we require, and the ways we organize information for the purposes of communication. Unfortunately, one of the great illusions of the so-called information age is that more information results in better decisions. Thus, we assume that the way to change people's minds is to bombard them with more information. If they haven't learned to create their own context as a frame of reference to help them select the information that will answer their questions, much of it will whiz by them and they are likely to end up victims of someone else's thought control.

Thompson sixth grade social studies teacher Doug Lakin describes how one of his students used the the same information that everyone else had to reach his own reasoned conclusion, a conclusion that moved beyond the either/or nature of the question. As the closing activity in a study of ancient Greece, his class conducted a debate on the relative merits of living in Sparta or Athens. Teams gathered their data, prepared their presentations, listened to their fellow students, and then wrote their personal conclusions. While most student picked Athens as the better city in which to live, Steve wrote:

> I have no opinion on this matter. Each city-state had a different purpose and focus. It is seemingly impossible to compare two things that have nothing in common. I do feel, however, Sparta was a less complete city-state than Athens. Athens had a good balance of education, politics, and warfare. Sparta was all warfare. They gave no thought to education.

They only cared about winning wars and being the best, and in the end, they ended up getting crushed anyway. That's dumb.

To summarize, "In the Information Context we emphasize concepts, integration, and connectedness; emphasize a systems approach to selecting, organizing, and processing information; incorporate the use of higher-order skills in addressing questions; and focus on the quality of information rather than the quantity.... Different information means different things to different people" (Goetz and Janz 1987).

The Ecosystem Context

The focus of the *Ecosystem Context* or *Global Context* — the fourth contextual relationship that informs and, thus, forms us — is our relationship to the physical world. Here we confront our relationship to the natural world — ranging from flowers and birds to the air we breathe and the food we eat. Here we also come face to face with our relationship to the man-made world of computers and automobiles, oil spills and nuclear weapons. It is here that we are able to explore the nature of the infinite network of relationships that connect the two worlds of nature and culture. Rather than being two separate systems that interact at specific points, e.g., forests and oceans, the reality is that human culture is inextricably embedded in a vast network of interlocking, interdependent ecological systems of air, water, and soil that sustain all life on earth. One consequence of our embeddedness in this dynamic, systemic network of relationships is that everything we do makes a difference.

The Ecosystem Context is where I experience the *external, physical limits* within which I encounter reality. Because the Earth's ecological systems — which we euphemistically call "the environment" — provide the air, water, food, and shelter that are absolutely necessary for life, they are literally *the life support systems of the planet.* As such, they represent very real and pragmatic limits upon which our collective survival depends. From this perspective, the Earth ecosystem provides us with the "big picture" context that shapes and will ultimately determine the success or failure of life on earth. Although in one way or another these ecological realities pattern and govern everything we do, most of us are totally ignorant of them. The irony is that this ignorance is a relatively new phenomenon. Prior to World War II, most Americans lived in rural environments — as did most of the world's people. As a result, humans were far more familiar with and sensitive to ecological realities that we are today. Now, compounding the potential damage created by or resulting from our ignorance of these fundamental principles, there is the technological capability for massive ecological destruction such as that being perpetuated in the Amazon rainforests and, though to a lesser degree, in our own country. Fritjof Capra (1993) reminds us that "our ignorance of ecology is one of the root causes of the economic and social crises of our time." To refer to this contextual relationship as the Global Context is to be reminded of the global nature of these interdependent systems and the dilemmas that threaten their integrity.

When Ruth Ann Dunton's sixth grade students at Thompson were asked to suggest laws that would govern a society dedicated to global cooperation, their answers demonstrated that sixth graders are perfectly capable of understanding the ecological constraints and global implications of living in today's world. After much discussion in their cooperative teams, the class came up with the following list.

- No pollution.
- Only ten trees per person can be cut in any given year. And when a tree is cut down it is replaced by two others.
- Only police can have guns.
- Animals can be killed only for food, never for fun.
- *All* garbage must be recyclable and recycled.
- No smoking.
- No racism.
- No homeless people.
- No deadly auto exhausts.
- No one with more power than anyone else.
- Equal justice for everyone.
- No one is illiterate.

- No more manufacturing of nuclear weapons.

- Wars are outlawed.

- More equity in the tax laws.

Even third graders can understand some of the implications of the Ecosystem Context. Following a district-wide workshop that I conducted on systems thinking, third grade teacher Ellen Smith introduced her students to a study of wind and air. Each student made a paper globe as a starting place for learning how wind and air circulate. This led into a broader discussion of various forms of pollution and concluded with the insight — demonstrated in a concrete way with their paper globes — that "there is no such place as away." By the end of the study, all of the students had gotten their parent's agreement to start home recycling programs.

To summarize, "In the Ecosystem Context we emphasize a global perspective; recognize limits; stress the ecological concepts of interdependence, diversity, change, competition/cooperation, adaptation, cycles, and energy flow; and stress the organic nature of Planet Earth and all its systems, including cultural and knowledge systems" (Goetz and Janz 1987).

Designing a Contextual Curriculum

Context is only one feature of an integrated curriculum. Before I discuss the remaining elements, it will be helpful to look at how the various components of an integrated curriculum fit together. Figure 4-1 provides a "big picture" overview that can be used as a conceptual blueprint. First, it identifies the seven elements that I consider to be basic to an integrated curriculum. Second, it suggests a step-by-step design strategy that will be particularly useful for the first time curriculum designer.

The first three "steps" of the process are philosophical. Without this theoretical context, the steps that follow become just another rather elaborate way of organizing information. However, because there is nothing more practical than a good theory, these initial stages may well be the most important in the entire design process. Each of these stages has been discussed in depth in the previous chapters.

The next three steps are actual "design" stages where teachers begin to identify the context of a topic by an appropriate use of concepts and questions. The final component is not really a stage at all because the learning community may already be in existence when the decision is made to integrate the curriculum. For example, at Thompson Middle School, several of the grade-level teams have already developed many of the characteristics of a learning community (see final chapter) prior to their first curriculum integration workshop. In this case, the learning community provided the soil within which the integrated curriculum was able to thrive and flower. However, for other schools and classrooms, the curriculum design process itself may be the means by which learning communities come into being. The important point is that by its very nature, a learner-centered integrated curriculum will be embedded in a learning community.

Before I discuss each of these seven components, I want to make one final comment about the blueprint in Figure 4-1. It is important to remember that any linear process has its inherent limitations. Once one has fully embraced the philosophical/theoretical context described above, designing a curriculum is a dynamic, systemic process that calls for greater flexibility and adaptability than is possible with linear, step-by-step procedures. In Chapter Seven I describe the dynamic nature of this process as it was used with one of the teams at Thompson Middle School.

1. *An integrated curriculum begins with an assumption of "the connectedness of things."* As I have already noted, this elemental assumption is essential to our understanding of the integrated curriculum. Without an appropriate philosophical context, any efforts to redesign the curriculum will fail. As has happened so many times before, the sheer force of custom and inertia will prevail and things will return to the status quo.

2. *An integrated curriculum is learner-centered.* Learning is "meaning-making." In order to create meaning, we are constantly making connections, identifying patterns, and organizing bits of knowledge, experience, and behavior into meaningful wholes. However, while I can share my thoughts, my ways of putting ideas together, my meaning — as I am doing through this book — I cannot create meaning for anyone else. In the end, each of us as learners must create our own meanings. We will do this by making our own connections, by identifying the patterns and relationships that make sense to us, and then organizing the ideas in ways that satisfy

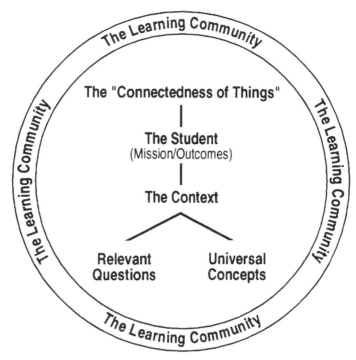

Figure 4-1. Designing an Integrated Curriculum

our needs and goals. Genuine learning comes only when I stand at the center and take ownership of the process.

3. *An integrated curriculum is mission-driven.* The goal of learning — expressed as a mission statement — represents the vision — the dream — the ultimate objective. This mission serves as both a lodestar and an inspiration, providing both direction and motivation. It should go without saying that the mission must honor the centrality of the learner and reflect his or her real-life needs.

4. *An integrated curriculum is contextual.* To conclude the discussion above, I will only note here that when I use the term *context* I am referring to *the frame of reference that provides meaning.* When there is no context, there is no meaning. Facts presented as they are in most schools are essentially meaningless. Their only practical value may be in a friendly game of Trivial Pursuit, or to pass a test — that is, a not-so-friendly game of Trivial Pursuit. If learning is to be meaningful, it must incorporate context.

5. *An integrated curriculum focuses on relevant questions.* Context is

created and explored in two ways — through questions and through concepts. In Chapter Five I will focus on "questions worth arguing about." These are essential questions that are relevant to the life experience of the learner. While traditional curriculum too often seeks to answer questions no one is asking, an integrated curriculum focuses on the learner's questions that reflect real-life interests.

Questions are designed to focus attention on the four contextual relationships discussed above. Using the various subject areas as resources in service of a central Focus Question, the contextual questions provide *horizontal integration*, that is, integration among the various subjects. The primary criterion for selecting the contextual questions to be explored is their relevance to the focus question.

6. *An integrated curriculum is framed by a set of universal principles and concepts.* Concepts also reflect context. In Chapter Six I will suggest a set of universal concepts that are relevant to all subject areas and can be used as a cognitive framework for learning more detailed information in any of these areas. Because of their widespread relevance, these concepts become powerful bridges across which ideas, principles, and experiences learned in one area can be adapted and applied in many other areas — the transfer of learning. These concepts can be revisited over and over again, each time with increased insight and meaning.

When these universal concepts are used to frame the curriculum at several grade levels simultaneously, they provide *vertical integration*, or integration across grade levels. This is the basis for the so-called spiral curriculum, where the same concepts are explored in many different contexts, year after year.

7. *An integrated curriculum is shared by a "community of learners."* According to indigenous wisdom, it takes a village to raise a child. In like manner, it takes a community of learners to educate a child — or an adult. Community, however, requires more than proximity. Just because teachers and students spend six hours a day together, doesn't make them a community of learners. It is difficult for classrooms and schools that give priority to competition, individual achievement, and personal success to generate a genuine sense of community. The need to design schools and classrooms

as authentic learning communities may be one of the most pressing needs in education. This will be discussed in more detail in Chapter Eight.

Having identified the systemic process by which one can design an integrated curriculum, it is instructive to look at the primary attributes that characterize an integrated, learner-centered curriculum. Remember that the following characteristics reflect priorities of emphasis, not either/or options.

An integrated, learner-centered curriculum gives priority to:

- context over content

- concepts over facts

- questions over answers

- imagination over knowledge

- intuition over rational logic

- developmental intent over graded content

- the learning process over the product of learning

- quality of information over quantity of information.

Conclusion

Human beings seek meaning like ducks seek water. Anyone who has observed children at play knows the kind of meaning they inject into objects or situations that, to the observer, mean something quite different. A piece of paper becomes an airplane, a saucepan becomes a boat, a storybook character becomes an intimate friend. Daydreaming is another important way children — romantics by nature — make their own meaning. They imagine themselves in Walter Mitty fashion as explorers and heros or a hundred and five other marvelous and exciting ways of being in the world. Or, lying atop a hill on a summer's day, they may just let their minds wander "lonely as a cloud that floats on high o'er vales and hills." In short, children are masters of creating contexts of meaning that suit their needs.

Then they enter school, which, as psychologist Charles Tart (1994) reminds us, "isn't primarily about education — but a brainwashing into the dominant ways of thinking which characterize our particular culture."

They are soon inundated with information that *other people* think is important for them to learn. In order to survive, they soon learn the rules, the chief
of which is to *remember everything the teacher says*. There is little time left for
looking out the window or for any other form of "learning through meaning-making." No longer free to create their own context in hundreds of
imaginative ways, children have little choice but to accept without question
the teacher's context and the meaning. They accept that the purpose of
learning is to pass tests; that the name of the game is competition; that real
success means being number one; that others are best qualified to grade
you; that sitting quietly and paying attention pays off; that most questions
are stupid; that mistakes are costly; that imagination is childish, silly, and a
waste of time; that life is run by clocks; and finally, that you can't beat the
system!

By the time our children grow up, they are ready to take their place in
society as productive workers — a role for which they have been well
prepared — at least until recently. Now, however, 80% of them don't like
their jobs but can't imagine an alternative. When they turn on the radio or
TV they are still inundated with information — sound bytes that have as
little meaning as the facts presented in school. But they have learned the
lessons of school well — let others create the contexts of meaning that will
guide their work, shape their ideas and relationships, and determine their
contributions to society. Since they don't really know what they want to do,
they don't know what to look for or what questions to ask. Thus, as Naisbitt
suggests, most of the information that comes their way each day whizzes
by them. What is remembered makes it easy to answer *someone else's* questions and think the way *they* want you to think.

A caricature? Of course. And yet, it's certainly one way of explaining
the almost overwhelming sense of apathy, powerlessness, futility, frustration, and anger that seem to pervade our society. What is needed, perhaps
most of all, is the realization that there are alternatives, that we do have
choices — and one of the most important choices we make is how we
educate our children.

Chapter Five

Questions Worth Arguing About

If *they* can keep you from asking the right questions they don't have to be concerned about your answers. (Thomas Pynchon)

One of the methodological foundations of science lies in the avoidance of the most fundamental questions. It is characteristic of physics to never really ask what matter is, biology not to really ask what life is, or for psychology not to ask what the soul is. (C. F. Von Weizsaecker)

During my first workshop at Thompson Middle School in the summer of 1991, I asked the *teachers* to identify the real-life questions that their students were asking. After some discussion they agreed on the following seven: Who am I? What are my legal rights? Why must I learn this? How will I be graded and why are grades important? How do I relate to my peers? How do I juggle the expectations of so many teachers?

I then asked, "How does what you are currently teaching address these questions?" The silence that followed was, as they say, deafening!

Later a colleague, Carole Cooper, visited a number of classrooms where she asked *students* to write down some of the questions that they were most concerned about. It is significant that none were trivial questions.

What is even more significant is that their concerns are both personal and social, local and global. This is just a sampling of students' responses: "What will I be when I grow up?" "What will the next war be about?" "Is there going to be enough room for landfills?" "Why am I here?" "Will the ozone layer get thinner?" "When will racism end?" "Will there be another depression?" "Can we help all of the suffering people?" "Can we save the rainforest?" "Will I succeed?" "How can I get along with my parents?" "What will the future be like?"

The late MIT physicist Jerrold Zaccharias once defined education as "the raising of questions worth arguing about." These students' questions certainly fit this characterization. Any one of them could be the starting point for a semester's course of study. It should be obvious that the most effective way to educate anyone is to ask the kinds of provocative questions that elicit the interests of the learner and motivate them to seek answers that satisfy their needs. This simple, yet profound truth may well lie at the heart of what ails education today. In our efforts to analyze, manipulate, and formalize the teaching and learning processes, we have forgotten that *"Nothing shapes our lives so much as the questions we ask — or refuse to ask"* (Keen 1994). Perhaps the reason is that in our product-oriented culture where answers are so important, we have forgotten the art of asking tough, sticky, value-laden questions.

Michael Ray and Michelle Myers, in their book *Creativity in Business* (1986) based on their pioneering course at Stanford's distinguished Graduate School of Business, devote an entire chapter to the topic, "Ask Dumb Questions."

> You'll soon become adept at knowing a dumb question when you hear it. You'll recognize it by the answers it generates. A dumb question creates explosions, concatenations, cascades of insights ... a dumb question is not *dead-ended, etiquette-oriented, accusatory, or shallow.*

These are the questions that one Nobel laureate called "jugular questions" that reach the essence of things. They're the kind of off-the-wall questions that a four-and-a half year-old named Scott asked in less than an hour: What's behind a rainbow? — What color is the inside of my brain? — What's inside of a rock? A tree? A sausage? Bones? My throat? A spider? — Does the sky have an end to it? If it doesn't, how come you can see it? — Why are my toes in front of my feet?" (Ray and Myers 1986).

One example of a dumb question suggested by Ray and Myers is pretty basic: "What is a question?" Michelle Ray who has spent her life examining the nature of questions, offers the following suggestions.

- A question is an opening to creation.

- A question is an unsettled and unsettling issue.

- A question is an invitation to creativity.

- A question is a beginning of adventure.

- A question is seductive foreplay.

- A question is a disguised answer.

- A question pokes and prods that which has not yet been poked and prodded.

- A question is a point of departure.

- A question has no end and no beginning.

- A question wants a playmate.

It is clear that we are not discussing the kinds of questions that one usually hears in school. Indeed, I think it is safe to say that because of the linear, cause-and-effect logic of our schooling, when we think of questions, most of us immediately assume not only that there is an answer — but a right answer. I think there must be a correlation between the emphasis in education on right answers and the fact that as a society, we seem to have lost the art of asking open-ended, provocative questions worth arguing about. But as Robert Sternberg, IQ theorist of Yale University, points out, intelligence includes the ability to ask appropriate questions, a capacity that is apparently fundamental to higher-order thinking (Sternberg 1987).

It is sad but true that conventional wisdom at all levels of our educational system from kindergarten through graduate school holds that teachers never ask questions they don't know the answer to. The result — as noted earlier — is that too many teachers spend most of their time providing answers to questions students never ask.

I suspect that one reason elementary science has been so poorly taught is the fear teachers have of questions that they can't answer. In an age of specialization, few elementary teachers consider themselves scientists. As a result, they teach only the most elementary facts, which elicit few if any questions. Of course, teachers may not always be able to control the questions that pop into the minds of their students. I often ask teachers how they handle off-the-wall questions that seem to have little, if any, obvious relevance to the topic being discussed. The truth is that as kids get older, most learn very quickly the kinds of questions that are allowed and those that may elicit a response like: "Where in the world did you think of that question?" — "We're not talking about rainbows — or trees — or sausages — or bones — or ...."

And yet, one of the most endearing, and sometimes frustrating characteristics of little — and sometimes not so little — children is their ability to ask questions. Beginning at an early age, they are full of questions about everything from "What makes flowers yellow?" to "Where do the stars come from?" "Where does God live?" Where did I come from?" Ted Sizer calls these life's "essential questions" and argues that these are the grist for learning. However, almost as soon as children begin formal schooling, their questions cease and by the sixth grade, teachers are convinced that their students don't know enough to ask intelligent questions. It is obvious that teachers who disparage students like this are not ready to design a curriculum around students' questions and concerns. But teachers can learn, as members of one sixth grade team at Thompson discovered to their surprise.

Having resisted curriculum changes for almost three years, the team decided to invite me to help plan their year-end program — the only all-team activity of the year. Ostensibly, this was to be an integrative, learner-centered endeavor. For two hours I kept asking questions and suggesting alternative ways of organizing the "content" of the activity — apparently to no avail. Prodding for some glimmer of flexibility was like pulling teeth. I left the room feeling both frustrated and discouraged. Imagine my surprise a few days later when the principal called to tell me that the team had really enjoyed our time together and felt it had been very worthwhile. I heard nothing more until the following fall when one of the team members stopped me in the hall and told me that the activity had been the best and most rewarding they had ever had. What amazed her most were the *questions the students had asked, their eagerness and excitement about exploring those questions, and the depth of learning that resulted.*

Historically, education has reflected the agenda of the adult world rather than the agenda of the child's world. And, perhaps to some degree, that is necessary. But, as in most other cases, the issue is seldom "either/or" but rather "both/and." For example, Jerome Bruner (1960) points out that most basic concepts and general ideas can be made relevant to children in some way at any age. The operative word is *relevance*. Unless the content of the curriculum matches the intent of the growing organism we call the child, the results are unpredictable and can even be chaotic, e.g., high school dropouts who complete their schooling by earning what Bob Samples (1993) calls a "Ph.D. in street smarts." When there is an appropriate "fit" between content and nature's developmental plan, the child's enthusiasm and capacity for thinking and learning seems to know no bounds. In short, while the content may be selected by the adult, the clues as to its appropriateness not only must, but I believe, can come from the child. After all, in the final analysis, it is the child's curiosity rather than the adult's desire to provide answers that will direct and shape the successful curriculum.

Learning to Ask Questions Worth Arguing About

In the absence of textbooks — except as possible resources — and in light of the sheer amount of knowledge and information available to teachers and students alike, it may be difficult for teachers — and, hopefully, students and teachers working together — to decide what knowledge and information is most important to achieve the desired learning outcomes. The Contextual Matrix (See Figure 5-1) helps teachers determine the relevant knowledge and information appropriate to a given area of study. At the same time, the Matrix is a powerful cognitive model for organizing the curriculum to graphically depict both the interrelatedness of these contextual perspectives and the unique focus of each. The Matrix can be used at any level in a single subject, or with several subjects. It has also been used effectively in both personal and organizational settings where people wanted to create and explore their own contexts of meaning.

In order to understand the relevance of these four contextual relationships to a given topic or situation, we need to ask the appropriate questions: questions that are open-ended and have no absolute right or wrong answers. These are not questions that invite polarized, yes/no answers like

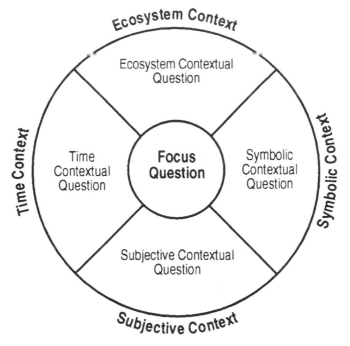

Figure 5-1. The Contextual Matrix

the questions around which academic debates are organized. Instead of seeking factual answers, these questions reflect a search for meaning. In short, they are contextual questions.

Focus Questions

The first step in designing a program of study or exploration —
euphemistically called a curriculum unit — is to select a Focus Question. As its name implies, this question captures the essence of the study, is necessarily broad in scope, and provides the directions that will be pursued. Implicit in the Focus Question are the anticipated outcomes. When the Focus Question reflects a preestablished theme, e.g., the human body, it might be something like, *"How does the human body work?"* When the Focus Question reflects a proposed exploration of students' real-life experiences, it might be *"What does it mean to grow up in today's world?"*

In an inner-city district where I conducted workshops, the ninth grade students were required to study John Steinbeck's novel, *The Red Pony*, the story of a boy growing up on a Montana ranch. Forced to teach a novel that, based on her previous experience, seemed to be totally irrelevant to the lives of her predominately Black students, the teacher decided to redesign the study using a Contextual Matrix. By selecting as a Focus Question, *"What does it mean to grow up in today's world?"* and eliciting her students' responses to this question, she created a context for the novel that was relevant to their lives, and in doing so, captured both their interest and their imagination. Not only was it the first time everyone had read the entire book without pressure from her, they eagerly extended their study beyond the Montana ranch to other sections of the country as well, in each case using an appropriate novel as the basis for further exploration.

Focus questions can be used within a discipline to turn what was once a content-centered unit into an integrated one. For example, a high school science teacher designed an entire semester's class around the question *"How will genetic engineering affect human life in the future?"* Students spent the first week reading and discussing the science fiction novel *Where Late the Sweet Birds Sang* by Kate Wilhelm (1976). In addition, they read as much as they could find about genetic engineering and biomedical technology in newspapers, magazines, and other materials supplied by the teacher and the resource center. By the end of the week, they had enough information and knowledge to begin formulating the questions that teams of students would explore during the ensuing weeks. From time to time as appropriate, the teacher presented mini-lectures, but always in response to the readiness of the students. Periodically, students would report on their findings to the class. These reports were always followed by in-depth discussions in "jigsaw teams" — temporary dialogue groups composed of one person from each of three of four study teams. As students became more sophisticated in their insights and knowledge, deeper and more "professional" questions began to emerge — many of which focused on the social, economic, political, and ecological ramifications of genetic engineering. The open-ended essay on the final exam (required by the district) provided ample opportunity for students to summarize and synthesize what they had learned during the semester. Needless to say, the grades were the best she had ever seen in what traditionally had been viewed as a tough class.

A ninth grade history teacher designed an introductory course on U.S. history around the question, "How has the natural landscape shaped

American history?" Another high school teacher used as a Focus Question for an Introduction to World History, "What makes a culture 'civilized'?" A college professor used as a starting point for an Introduction to Philosophy course the Focus Question, "What is philosophy?" Social studies classes are ideal vehicles for integrating the various subject areas into a single focus. For example, another high school teacher designed an interdisciplinary unit around the question, "What do the various disciplines tell us about war?" An eighth grade civics teacher designed an integrated course on the U.S. Constitution around the question, "How is the Constitution a systemic model for a democratic society?"

When a teacher or a team of teachers wants to design a fully integrated program of study that ranges far and wide and incorporates several subject areas, broader questions are more appropriate. The following grade-level Focus Questions were used by the United Catholic Parochial School in Beaver Dam, Wisconsin, to design an integrated K-8 curriculum.

Grade One: How big is my neighborhood?

Grade Two: How am I a member of many families?

Grade Three: What makes communities work?

Grade Four: How does the world work?

Grade Five: What is culture?

Grade Six: What does it mean to be human?

Grade Seven: How do systems work? What is our relationship to the Earth?

Grade Eight: How does one live responsibly in the global community?

Contextual Questions

After the Focus Question has been identified, the next step is to find Contextual Questions that focus attention on the appropriate relationship. Sometimes it may be useful to have more than one question for a relationship. These questions focus and frame the exploration, capture the essence of each contextual relationship, and may serve to highlight one or more aspects of that relationship. Some of the Contextual Questions below were designed by the parochial school faculty. The rest come from other sources.

As might be expected, there are obvious similarities among questions at the different levels. However, since the focus or context of each is different, e.g., family and community, essentially they are different questions.

First grade focus question: How big is my neighborhood?

The Subjective Context: What is my neighborhood? How many neighborhoods do I belong to?

The Time Context: How has my neighborhood changed?

The Symbolic Context: Who are my neighbors and how are their families like my family and different from my family?

The Ecosystem Context: How does nature affect my neighborhood?

Second grade focus question: How am I a member of many families?

The Subjective Context: Who am I? How am I alike and different from other children? How many families do I belong to? How is my body like a family?

The Time Context: Where did I come from? How does my body change? When will I become more independent?

The Symbolic Context: What kinds of families are there? In what ways are families alike? Different?

The Ecosystem Context: How do different families relate to the Earth? How do families use the Earth's resources? How do plants and animals and people live together?

Third grade focus question: What makes communities work? (Figure 5-2)

The Subjective Context: How is my life influenced by my community? In what ways do I communicate with others? What communities do I belong to?

The Time Context: How do human communities grow and change? How do natural communities grow and change? What can we learn from patterns of change?

The Symbolic Context: What makes a community? What kinds of communities are there? What are the rules that communities live by?

The Ecosystem Context: What can we learn from natural communities? How can communities preserve natural resources?

Figure 5-2. Contextual Matrix: What Makes Communities Work?

Fourth grade focus question: How does the world work?

The Subjective Context: What are the rules/limits I have to live by? What kind of rules do I set for myself? Why do different people have different rules?

The Time Context: How have the rules/limits by which humans live changed over time? What kind of rules/limits will we need in the future?

The Symbolic Context: How have humans discovered and created the rules/limits we live by? What are the patterns to be found in human rules/limits? In natural rules/limits?

The Ecosystem Context: What are the rules/limits that make natural systems work? What happens when we don't follow nature's rules/limits?

Fifth grade focus question: What is culture?

The Subjective Context: How does my culture influence my life? What is my culture?

The Time Context: How have humans and cultures changed over time? What will cultures look like in the future?

The Symbolic Context: What is culture? How are cultures similar and how are they different?

The Ecosystem Context: In what ways are cultures and ecosystems interdependent? How have cultures been influenced and shaped by their land?

Sixth grade focus question: What does it mean to be human? (Figure 5-3)

The Subjective Context: Who am I? Where do I belong? How do I relate to family, peers, strangers? How am I star stuff? How do I know myself?

The Time Context: Where did I come from? Where did humans come from? How did life begin? What is the origin of the human species? What is my personal history? Where am I going? What do I want to be/do when I become an adult? What is the future of the human species? What is time?

The Symbolic Context: How do humans communicate with each other? How do humans know? How do I think and learn? How does the human perceive information? How does language influence and shape the way we

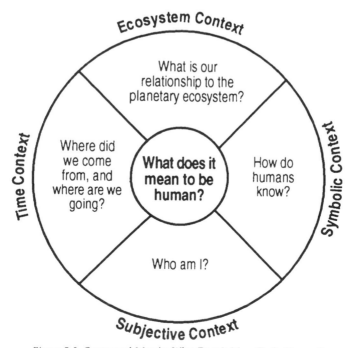

Figure 5-3. Contextual Matrix: What Does It Mean To Be Human?

think? What is the effect of technology on how we perceive, organize, and communicate information?

The Ecosystem Context: What is our relationship to the planetary ecological systems? What is my personal relationship to these systems? How are we responsible to and for living and non-living things? How do human societies interact with living and non-living things on the planet?

Seventh grade focus question: How do systems work? What is our relationship to the Earth?

The Subjective Context: How does my body work as a system? How do I depend on the Earth? What is my relationship to the Earth? How do I use natural resources?

The Time Context: How has human's relationship to the Earth changed over time? What will it be in the future?

The Symbolic Context: How do natural systems function? What are the patterns that are similar in human and natural systems?

The Ecosystem Context: What can we learn from natural systems? What are the natural constraints that humans must learn to live with?

Eighth grade focus question: How does one live responsibly in the global village? (See Figure 5-4)

The Subjective Context: In what ways am I a citizen of the global village? How does living in a global village influence my daily life? What are my obligations to other members of the global village?

The Time Context: What can we learn from our past that will help us understand how to live peacefully in the global village? What kind of goals or rules should exist for global citizens?

The Symbolic Context: In what ways is the global community a village? What are the rules for village and community living? How can we create global channels of communication through which knowledge and information can be shared freely? What are the barriers that keep us from communicating with each other? What role do other "languages" such as mathematics, computer language, art, and music play in shaping the ways we — as individual or nations — relate to each other?

The Ecosystem Context: What are the ecological constraints that must

Figure 5-4. Contextual Matrix: How Does One Live Responsibly in a Global Community?

shape life in the global village? What are the ecological principles that can guide decision-making? What can we learn from ecological communities that can help us create more effective local and global communities?

Expanding the Contextual Matrix with Perspective Questions

So far, all of the Contextual Matrixes have been the simpler models that include only Focus and Contextual Questions. The Matrix can also incorporatePerspective Questions. This expanded Matrix (See Figures 5-5 and 5-6) is particularly useful when the intent is to explore a Focus Question from the perspective of several academic disciplines. Initially, teachers at Thompson used this more inclusive, interdisciplinary Matrix. However, they soon found that the more questions they identified, the more they were preempting students' questions. The second year they unanimously decided to use the simpler matrix, which was in fact designed by Doug Thompson, an eighth grade team leader. Figure 5-7 is an example of a matrix created by the three eighth grade teams working cooperatively. In addition

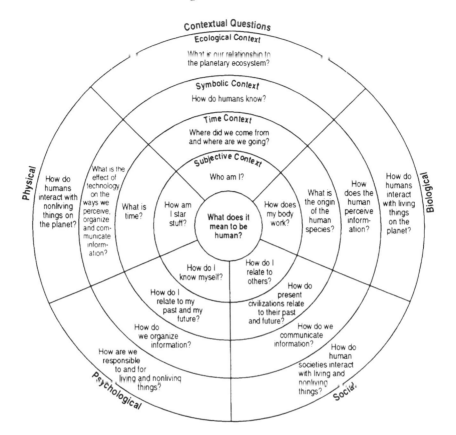

Figure 5-5. Contextual Matrix with Perspective Questions: "What Does It Mean to be Human?"

to the questions, this matrix includes the concepts that are relevant to the questions (See Chapter 6).

Several of the Focus Questions above could be used at the high school level where departmentalization makes most forms of an integrated curriculum difficult if not impossible. For example, the Focus Question, "What does it mean to be human?" has been used to design an interdisciplinary curriculum at several different grade levels and, in its expanded form (Figure 5-5) could also be an effective organizing question for an interdisciplinary high school curriculum at any grade level. In the same way, an entire high school curriculum could be organized around the question, "How does one live responsibly in the global community?" using questions such as those in Figure 5-6.

Indeed, questions like these can be revisited periodically through a

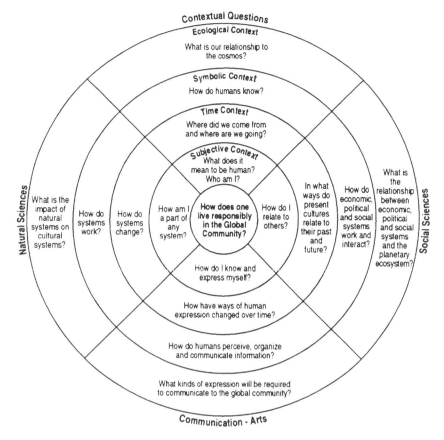

Figure 5-6. Contextual Matrix with Perspective Questions:
"How Does One Live Responsibly in the Global Community?"

student's entire school career, each time eliciting from students more penetrating questions and expanded sophistication of understanding.

Student Questions

One concern that has been raised is the degree to which the curriculum is designed around teachers' rather than students' questions. As Bill O'Hagan and Sharon Mulcahy discovered (See Chapter 3), the two are not mutually exclusive. While one can make the case that in an ideal situation, all of the questions are generated by students, realistically teachers are limited by the constraints of content requirements and their own comfort levels. However, when the initial Matrix is created by one or more teachers, it is important that student questions be elicited as soon as possible. It is

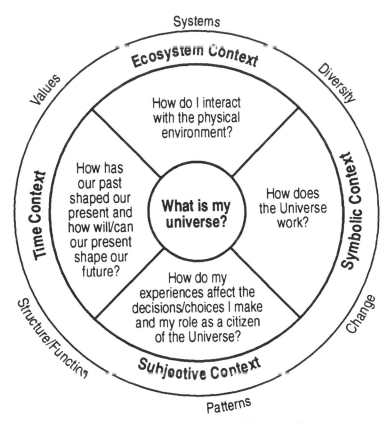

Figure 5-7. Eighth Grade Team Contextual Matrix and Concepts

also important for the students to discuss the Focus and Contextual Questions both as a whole class and in small teams. This assures that everyone understands the questions; it also provides an opportunity to expand the students' horizons prior defining the specific questions they want to study. Then students are invited to identify their own questions vis-à-vis the particular question that will be the next focus of study. After all the student questions have been identified, the whole class can participate in sorting and synthesizing the questions into a few general questions. These then become the focus for cooperative team exploration.

Once students become involved in exploring their own questions, one of the not so surprising consequences is noted by Resource Center Director, Chris Sherman, "Kids are generating questions and then staying on-task in the LRC. They aren't just copying from encyclopedias any more."

Conclusion

My experience at Thompson has taught me that major change is not easy and that most teachers can apply these new ideas only incrementally. For example, many teachers still prefer to organize curriculum around topics and theme rather than questions. As I noted above, this seems to reflect a still strong attachment to a particular content that, for whatever reason, the teacher considers to be important. They are comfortable with themes — holiday, seasons, countries — and it is difficult to wean them from such seemingly innocuous habits. Does it really make a difference?

This debate will continue because, like most other ideas, there is no single right way for everyone. However, I will continue to encourage the use of questions for two reasons. First, questions reflect the way we learn. By stimulating curiosity and interest, they can be highly motivating. The second reason is that the outcome is always implicit in the question. Because they focus attention on the outcome, questions provide greater direction to a unit than a theme. For example, it seems obvious that a thematic unit on Thanksgiving could be more focused and more motivating if it were organized around the question, "Why are the United States and Canada the only countries in the world to celebrate Thanksgiving?" Implicit in this question is the outcome — that students will understand the uniqueness of Thanksgiving as a North American holiday. Or to take an example from Donna Stockman's seventh grade team, which next year plans to integratively teach two units sequentially — the first on Systems, which will be followed by a unit on the Human Body. It seems to me that a provocative question like "How is my body like the Earth — or the Universe?" might integrate both units more fully and simultaneously generate a much wider range of questions from students. What would emerge in the process might be more challenging for both students and the teachers.

However, it seems to me that the important thing is not whether a given unit is designed around a theme or a question, but rather that the content of the unit reflects the questions students ask rather than the prepackaged material written by someone else. And, as we have seen, students can and, when given the opportunity, do ask questions well worth arguing about. And, as we have already seen, when they feel that their questions are important, students have no difficulty in identifying enough questions to fill any curriculum.

I remember a discussion about the use of questions with one of the high school history teachers at St. Charles High School. When I suggested that he could design his class around students' questions, he insisted that his students didn't even know enough to ask questions about the Civil War. When I asked what response he would receive if he asked his students what they wanted to know about the Civil War, he said the first question would probably be, "What was the Civil War?" My response was: "That's a good question to begin with, isn't it."

It seems to me that an astute teacher could well begin a unit by having students research that very basic question. As they began to get some insights, the study could be expanded into a full-blown unit that consisted only of student investigations, research, reports, etc. I think it could become a very exciting unit.

Good teaching is a matter of creating a context that not only allows but vigorously encourages students to become actively involved in their own learning. Good teaching is an art that requires sensitivity, humility, and an infinite confidence in the innate ability of kids to learn about the world in which they live. It's a matter of pointing the direction, turning it over to the learners and getting out of the way! Sam Keen provides us with a healthy reminder that with questions such as these, "in the beginning is the end" — both the answer and the process are implicit in the question.

Chapter Six

Concepts as Organizing Frameworks

> The mind thinks with ideas, not with information…. The principal task of education, therefore, is to teach young minds how to deal with ideas: how to evaluate them, extend them, adapt them to new uses. This can be done with the use of very little information, perhaps none at all…. An excess of information may actually crowd out ideas, leaving the mind (young minds especially) distracted by sterile, disconnected facts, lost among shapeless heaps of data. (Roszak 1994)

> The learning process requires that new information become part of a coherent conceptual structure, yet no systematic attempt is being made to create a curriculum which reflects that requirement. (Marion Brady 1989)

In Chapter Two I discussed the relationship between systems thinking, the structure of knowledge, and the fact that humans construct rather than discover knowledge. In this chapter I want to explore in greater detail the central function that concepts play in understanding and constructing knowledge. Although I have been using the terms *principle* and *concept* interchangeably, here I will use the term *concepts* since this is a term used extensively in education. Although there are many broad concepts that are discipline-specific, in general the concepts to which I will be referring are those universal, systemic principles that are implicit if not explicit in every academic discipline, e.g., *interdependence, diversity, structure/function.* Because these concepts can be applied in meaningful ways to every field of study, they suggest the interdependent nature of all forms of knowledge and provide powerful cognitive tools with which to bridge the chasms that exist between the various disciplines.

My working definition of concept is *a big idea that helps us makes sense of, or connect, lots of little ideas.* Concepts are like cognitive file folders. They provide us with a framework or structure within which we can file an almost limitless amount of information. One of the unique features of these conceptual files is their capacity for cross-referencing. Because concepts focus on similarities and homologies, they provide powerful linkages between what would otherwise be considered disparate and seemingly incompatible information. For example, think of how many "little ideas" from almost every field of knowledge can be linked together under the concept, "hot." Once a child learns experientially what "hot" means, she can make an almost infinite number of connections and associations without having to be burned again.

Because of their amazing capacities of association, concepts are *the primary cognitive information organizing strategies, and, as such, are the most powerful and therefore most useful cognitive tools available to us.* Most of us are completely unaware of how we use concepts. Symington and Novak (1982) remind us, "It is through the concepts we form, and the linkages we make between them, that we make sense of the world around us." Theodore Roszak (1994) echos this when he writes, "The mind thinks with ideas [or concepts], not with information [or facts]."

Bruner (1960) was referring to concepts when he discussed the role of structure in thinking and learning. He identified four essential functions that concepts perform in helping us organize our perceptions and understanding of the world.

1. *Concepts provide structure for a discipline.*

In every academic discipline there are a set of fundamental concepts and principles that constitute the conceptual structure of the discipline. In Chapter Two, I compared such concepts to the studs that frame a house.

While studs do not provide detailed information about either the rooms or the house, they do furnish an overview of the shape, size, and layout of the rooms and a structural schema of the entire house. In like manner, while concepts don't provide information about the details of a subject, they do make it possible to understand the relationships that exist within that discipline and how it functions as an integrated knowledge system. Based on the importance of understanding this structure, the National Center for Improving Science Education has proposed a set of conceptual themes for organizing science curriculum: "cause and effect, change and conservation, diversity and variation, energy and matter, evolution and equilibrium, models and theories, probability and prediction, structure and function, systems and interaction, and time and scale" (Brooks and Brooks 1993). Although these concepts represent fundamental scientific processes, from a systems perspective, they can be applied to other subjects as well.

Once a learner has grasped these relationships, she has a context for asking appropriate questions to find whatever information is required for a given task. In an age where we are swamped by information overload, to understand the conceptual structure of a subject is to literally know more with less information. This is why, to paraphrase the Chinese proverb, "a concept is worth a thousand — or perhaps ten thousand — facts." What an energy and time saver!

2. *Concepts provide a framework within which details can be more readily understood and remembered.*

The conceptual framework of a subject is a natural, built-in mnemonic. Once grasped, this structure provides a context-of-meaning for learning detailed information in the form of facts and data. Because what is being learned can be associated with what is already known, it becomes meaningful (i.e., "full of meaning") and can be remembered with relative ease. Gurley (1982) has demonstrated the degree to which concepts aid learning. In a ninth grade introductory Biology class, concepts and concept mapping were introduced as a structure for learning more detailed information (Figure 6-1). On a test administered *a year later*, the retention rate of the experimental group was 80% higher than the control group, which had been taught using the conventional method — beginning with facts independent of any conceptual framework.

3. Concepts are the primary bridges which make transfer of learning possible.

The transfer of learning is one of the most misunderstood concepts in education. Far from being a "science" that can be taught, as David Perkins and Gavriel Salomon (1992) suggest, the transfer of learning is an innate, intuitive capacity that is as natural as thinking and learning. Indeed, from what we now know about how thinking and learning take place, it seems clear that transfer is an integral feature of the cognitive process I have called intelligence/thinking/learning. The primary reason that so many adults are unable to transfer what has been learned in one situation to a different situation, is because they have been programmed to think linearly, inductively, and in little boxes.

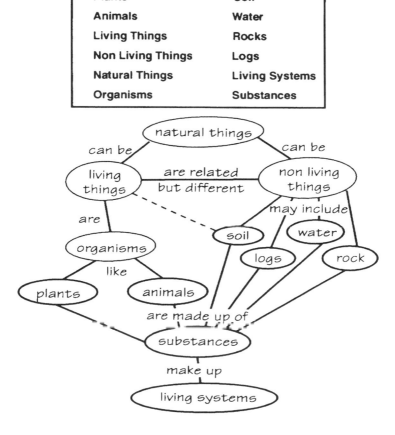

Plants	Soil
Animals	Water
Living Things	Rocks
Non Living Things	Logs
Natural Things	Living Systems
Organisms	Substances

Figure 6-1. Concept Map for a Biology Chapter

Hilda Taba points out that each academic discipline has its own array of distinctive facts which have little or no meaning within other fields of study. As long as learning focuses on these "facts as building blocks," no transfer of learning is possible because there are no natural bridges between the disciplines. As Taba's taxonomy of knowledge makes clear, the key to the transfer of learning is a conceptual framework that bridges the various disciplines and shows how things are related to each other. Since there are a number of fundamental concepts that all disciplines share, these concepts can provide the necessary bridges. For example, once a student learns the intrinsic relationship between *structure* and *function*, that insight can be applied in any arena, e.g., art, music, math, science, social studies, and language. In the same way, the other concepts identified by the National Center for Improving Science Education for organizing science curriculum — e.g., cause and effect, change and conservation, diversity and variation, energy and matter — are universally relevant. Once they are learned in science, they can be applied with meaning in virtually any subject.

Thompson School eighth grade team leader Doug Thompson notes that although members of the team were still teaching their own individual subjects, "The major strength for kids this year is that we are all talking about the same questions and concepts."

A second grade teacher found that her students quickly understood, with no more than two or three examples, the ecological concept, *adaptation*. Once they learned this, there were able to make intuitive leaps — what educators call the transfer of learning — to discover examples of adaptation in other areas, e.g., humans adapt to cold weather by building houses. To return to an illustration used earlier, consider the transfer of learning implicit in the many ways we use a term like "hot." Although few adults understand the physics of heat, we all know what is meant by "hot pants," "hot stock," "hot number," "hot tip," and "hot idea." Even children — who presumably aren't capable of abstract thinking — can generate a list of things that are or can be "hot." In addition to the more obvious things, "hot stove," "hot sun," "hot water," kids who have been raised on MTV may also talk about a "hot band" or a "hot song." This is because children naturally see relationships and make connections, often far beyond the capacities of adults who have been programmed to think in little boxes.

Kathy Krug's face glowed as she told us about how learning transfer occurred for one of her students. Warren had just finished reading a column from the *Chicago Tribune* in which columnist Bob Greene wrote about Michael Jordan's daily early morning drives to the Chicago White Sox training facility. Talking about his father who had been murdered the previous year, Jordan told Greene, "I'm alone in the car, but my father is with me.... I remember why I'm doing this. I remember why I'm here. I'm here for him." Warren's eyes sparkled. "Ms. Krug, Michael Jordan was just like Rudy Matt in the story we read last month, wasn't he!" (*Banner In The Sky* by Ramsey Ullman).

4. *Concepts provide the framework for lifelong learning.*

Twenty-five years ago Bruner suggested that concepts were the foundation for lifelong learning. With the focus today on preparing students to be lifelong learners, it is crucial for teachers to understand that one of the first steps toward achieving this outcome must be a recognition of the fundamental role that concepts play in thinking and learning. *Concepts help us make sense of our world precisely because they are the vehicles that carry most of the information necessary for thinking and learning.* To attempt to teach someone to think or learn without using concepts as a framework is like trying to teach them how to paddle without providing them with a canoe. Another, perhaps more accurate analogy is that concepts are like railroad tracks. Teaching facts without first understanding concepts is like trying to drive a locomotive without first laying out the tracks.

According to Brooks and Brooks (1993), there is a fifth function that concepts perform in the thinking/learning process: *They provide the cognitive framework that makes it possible for us to construct our own understandings of the world in which we live.* As has already been noted, whenever we learn something we place it into some framework that we already understand. In so doing, we create our own interpretation and meaning. Indeed, *learning is the act of interpretation that emerges from the interaction between the learner and the object of learning.* As C. T. Fosnot notes, "Learning is not discovering more, but interpreting through a different scheme or structure" (Brooks and Brooks 1993). In short, learning is "meaning-making" and requires a context (a cognitive structure) to occur. In order to aid and abet our natural capacity for constructing knowledge, the Brookses propose that teachers structure curriculum around primary concepts and "conceptual clusters of problems, questions, and discrepant situations."

Concepts and the Theory of Living Systems

Of immense importance in becoming a lifelong learner is an understanding of what are generally known as *systems principles* — broad concepts that, according to the theory of living systems, are universally applicable. Because these concepts apply to all fields of knowledge, they provide us with a single conceptual framework for thinking and learning and with a virtually unlimited number of cognitive bridges for the transfer of learning. To return to the railroad analogy, one set of tracks can carry trains of belonging to any railroad company.

According to physicist Fritjof Capra (1994),

The theory of living systems looks at the world in terms of relationships and integration. It recognizes that all life on earth is organized in an intricate web of inter-relationships. Far from being random, these relationships seem to be arranged in a series of complex, interconnecting patterns which we call living systems. *Whether we are describing individual organisms, social systems or ecological systems, these patterns are consistent, reflecting at all levels common properties and similar principles of organization.* (emphasis added)

These principles of organization are the principles of ecology. Although we tend to think of ecology as the study of nature's systems, the fact that human cultures are inextricably embedded in the these natural ecological systems, suggests that at some fundamental level, cultural systems are homologous — that is, "similar in structure and evolutionary origin" with natural systems. In short, cultural systems are ecological systems. As such, they may be considered subsystems of the planetary ecological system much the same way that the heart and lungs are subsystems of the human body. From this perspective, every academic discipline and professional field of work is ecological in character. For example,

- Sociology is the ecology of social groups.
- Political science is the ecology of collective decision-making.
- Economics is the ecology of finance and exchange.
- Anthropology is the ecology of culture.

- Business management is concerned with the ecology of organizations.

- Physics, chemistry, and geology are studies of the ecology of physical matter.

- Mathematics is the ecology of numbers and their relationship to physical matter.

- Reading and writing are fundamental expressions of the ecology of language and communication while art, music, drama, and dance reflect other, more subtle forms of the ecology of communication.

According to the theory of living systems, these academic disciplines share common properties and certain principles of organization with all other living systems from the simplest cell or organism to the global village. These are the principles and properties found in ecological systems.

Operating Principles for Living Systems

While there are hundreds of principles and concepts that characterize ecological systems, the primary ones include interdependence, sustainability, diversity, partnership, coevolution, fluctuating cycles, and energy flow. (Parts of the following descriptions are taken from Capra, Clark, and Cooper [1994].)

Interdependence. Interdependence is the unifying principle operative in all systems. As the first principle of ecology, it defines the nature of the complex web of relationships that exist among the individual parts of a system and between those parts and the system as a whole. Substantively, it is a relationship in which the success of the system as a whole depends upon the success of each individual member, just as the success of each member depends upon the success of the whole system. In ecology, this mutuality is best illustrated best by the relationship that exists between an ecological community and the individual niches which make up that community. Each niche represents a functional slot in the ecology of a community. In a food chain, for example, each species often has a highly specialized function: providing food for a predator species and at the same time acting as predator for the species on which it feeds. If a particular species is wiped out by disease, the stability of the entire ecological community is, to some degree, diminished. In the same way, each business in a small town community fills a unique niche. Anytime one of these businesses fails and is not replaced, the stability of the community is, to some extent, diminished. In both ecological and human communities, the success of these niches — whether species or business — depends upon the success of the community as a whole, while the success of the entire community depends upon the success of each niche.

Interdependence is a universal characteristic recognized as being fundamental to the success of all social, economic, and political systems. As an integrative concept, it can be applied with equal appropriateness to a work of art and the study of a galaxy; to writing a sentence and learning a language; to computer science and the engineering of a spaceship; to the sociology of a family or of a multinational corporation; to economics, political science, or ecology. Because of its comprehensive relevance, interdependence can become a powerful unifying strand in the broad tapestry of thinking and learning. Once a child understands what interdependence means, he or she is able, through the transfer of learning, to operationalize the concept in a virtually limitless number of applications.

Sustainability. Every system requires a resource base to provide the raw materials upon which the system depends for survival. Because every system is finite, its resource base is necessarily limited. The long-term survival (sustainability) of any system depends on its ability to live within these limits. While there are tolerances, there is always a point of no return beyond which a system cannot extend itself and recover. For example, in a severe drought an ecological community may be pushed beyond its capacity to recover.

These limited resources define the system's carrying capacity, i.e., its ability to sustain itself indefinitely on the given resources. A garden has a carrying capacity. So does a home, an office, a schoolroom, a business, a nation, and the planet. When the limits prescribed by available resources are exceeded, there is trouble. For example, just as an overcrowded garden is less productive, so crowding in an office inevitably cuts down on productivity. Crowding in a classroom always has negative consequences on learning. Crowding in our cities produces physical hazards — ranging from joblessness, homelessness, disease, and crime to more subtle psychological hazards, such as loneliness, stress, depression, anger, frustration, and powerlessness. These conditions are symptomatic of system disequilibrium — "dis-ease." While initially the symptoms may not be obvious, once they reach a critical mass, the result can be total systemic collapse, e.g., revolution.

Diversity. The successful maintenance and stability of any system depends substantially on the degree of complexity and diversity of its network of relationships. In general, the greater diversity results in greater stability. For example, an oak forest with its rich diversity of life is far more stable than a cornfield, which is essentially a monoculture. A natural forest is more stable than a man-made forest of Douglas firs planted by a lumber company. Stability in cultural systems also requires diversity. The diversity of ethnic and cultural backgrounds is one of the strengths of our nation. In spite of our envy of Japan's success, her major weakness is the lack of ethnic diversity. What appears to be strength may in time prove to be a fundamental weakness. It is ironic that both Japan and Germany, the two aggressor nations in World War II, were both in essence ethnic monocultures and highly susceptible to ideologies based on ethnic superiority. Such ideologies would have a harder time in the United States because if they appealed to one group (White supremacists), at the same time they would be rejected by many other groups. In all human organizations, diversity is necessary to maintain stability. This is especially important in our age of narrow specialization.

Partnership. All members of any living system are engaged in a subtle and dynamic interplay of competition and cooperation, involving countless forms of partnership strategies. These two powerful drives ideally function in a unique reciprocal relationship much like centrifugal and centripetal forces. When a dynamic balance between the two is achieved, the power and thrust of adaptive change results in both stability and creativity, each of which is crucial to the success of all living systems. When this balance is lost, the stability of the system is endangered. Too much competition leads to burnout and self-destruction. Too much cooperation leads to passivity, inertia, and apathy. The dynamic quality of this partnership principle is highlighted by the insight from chaos theory that it is at that elusive boundary between chaos and order where creativity and novelty emerge (Briggs and Peat 1989).

Competition is one of the most misunderstood of all ecological concepts. It is a dogma of capitalistic society that unbridled competition is the fundamental driving principle in the natural world. Extrapolating from this interpretation of natural principles, there is a powerful bias in our country toward unrestrained competition in human economies, i.e., social Darwinism. The irony is that a) there is no such thing as unrestrained competition in nature, and b) no one believes in unrestrained economic competition. In natural systems, competition within species is always constrained by cooperative strategies such as territoriality and dominance hierarchy. Competition between species is controlled by factors such as adaptive modifications, which often result in two similar species utilizing entirely different food sources. In cultural systems, the most vocal defenders of unrestrained economic competition are often the first to exploit political means to protect themselves from the very competition that they defend.

In short, competition apart from cooperation is essentially a meaningless concept. Even in so-called competitive sports, successful competition requires some form of cooperative behavior. Indeed, one cannot conceive of a game without rules, whether it be the "game of life" as played in nature or the economic game as played in both capitalist democracies and communist dictatorships.

Co-evolution. Change is a universal principle that reflects the impact of time on all systems. Systemic change occurs as species and groups coevolve through an interplay of creation and mutual adaptation. Ecosystems also coevolve with the larger systems of which they are a part. In each case, the *creative selection of novelty* in response to the changes in its environment is a fundamental property of life. This response is manifest in the process of change, growth, development, and learning and results in both creativity and increased diversity. The inability of a system to co-evolve eventually results in extinction — for a plant or animal species, for an indigenous culture, for a business, for a national government, for the human species.

Fluctuating Cycles. The interdependencies among the members of a system involve the exchange of information, i.e., matter and energy, in continuous cycles. These cycles act as feedback loops that make possible the healthy, dynamic balance required by the system. These cycles have the tendency to maintain themselves in a flexible, fluctuating state as they provide various levels of tolerance in the dynamic interplay between stability and change.

There are two kinds of cycles in natural and cultural systems. One is the rhythmic fluctuations that occur over time, such as the seasons, life cycles, and economic cycles. The other refers to the physical recycling of materials — the flow and exchange of atoms and molecules of matter through physical systems, such as the planetary ecological system and the human body, and the flow of money as a symbolic substitute for materials that flow through cultural systems. Cycles in living systems are never static. Rather, as rhythms of change, they reflect the ongoing adaptive processes of a system. Because of their dynamic nature, their function in living systems can be described best in cybernetic terms as information feedback loops. Just as urinalysis provides information/feedback about the health of the human body, the quality of our planetary water supply provides us with information/feedback about the health of our ecological systems. Historian Arthur M. Schlesinger, Jr. (1986), has identified a cyclical rhythm in our national life that oscillates between public purpose and private interest. He suggests that true cycles are self-generating, driven by their own internal rhythms. Each phase flows naturally from the conditions of the previous phase, and in turn, creates the conditions that call forth the next recurrence. In a similar manner, cycles are relevant to every subject studied in school and every arena in life. For example, power utility companies design their systems to account for peak and nonpeak loads. In the same way, we can apply our knowledge of how growth/rest cycles shape ecological systems to cultural systems such as economic or organizational systems, to make them more efficient. For example, burnout reflects a failure to apply what we know about growth/rest cycles to human and organizational systems.

Energy Flow. All living systems are open systems and as such are dependent upon an external energy source for survival. Just as our planetary ecology is dependent upon the energy from the sun, all plants and animals are dependent upon an external energy source in the form of food. If we were able to think of food as energy, we would learn to be as careful about the food we take into our bodies as we are about the quality of gasoline we use in our automobiles. Cultural systems depend for their survival upon an external form of energy called *information*. Money, knowledge, and data are all forms of energy transformed into information — energy in-formation — by the human mind. Just as the health of natural systems depends upon a free flow of solar energy throughout the system, so the health of cultural systems requires a free flow of information, e.g., money, knowledge, and data, throughout the system. System imbalance occurs whenever there is a glut of energy/information, e.g., money, in one part of a system at the expense of the rest of the system. If this becomes too pronounced, a systemic embolism may result.

While these are the major organizing principles that characterize living systems, there are a number of related concepts such as those recommended for science education, which are also universally applicable. Table 6-1 identifies some that are particularly useful in educational settings.

Table 6-1.
Ecological Principles and Concepts

Ecological Principles	Related Concepts
Interdependence	Community/Niche, Network, System Models
Sustainability	Carrying Capacity, Habitat, Limits
Diversity	Similarities and Differences, Stability
Partnership	Cooperation/Competition Structure/Function, Cause/Effect
Coevolution	Change, Adaptation, Succession, Values, Choice, Creativity
Energy Flow	Energy Exchange, Information Flow, Power
Fluctuating Cycles	Feedback, Cycles, Patterns, Balance, Permeable Boundaries, Tolerances

How Concepts Frame an Integrated Curriculum

Since all academic disciplines are in some elemental way ecological systems, these principles/concepts can be powerful cognitive organizers for framing an integrated curriculum that bridges all of the disciplines.

Because, as Bruner notes, these concepts can be taught in some way to children of all ages, they can be used to integrate a curriculum vertically, that is across grade levels. This is what Bruner meant by a "spiral curriculum" — one in which certain basic concepts are revisited year after year, each time with new information and insight. This is a far more powerful and natural means of articulation than that found in conventional curricula with its linear, often arbitrary progression of ideas, subjects, and themes from the simplest to the more sophisticated. Figure 6-2 shows how the K–8 grade level curricula discussed earlier could be integrated vertically using

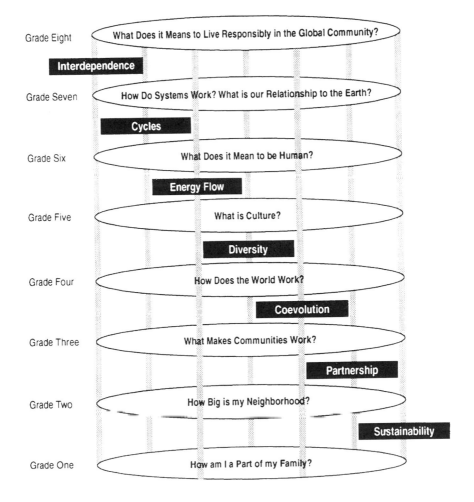

Figure 6-2. A K-12 Curriculum Framed by Seven Concepts

the ecological concepts.

I will illustrate how some of these concepts might be used with the Focus or Contextual Questions in Chapter Five. Because of their ability to facilitate inquiry and learning, questions are useful for directing attention to specific concepts and their relevance to Focus or Contextual Questions. As might be expected, many of the questions apply equally well to several Focus Questions, e.g., families, neighborhoods, and communities.

Focus Question: How Am I a Member of Many Families?

- What are the similarities and differences among the members of your family? What would it be like to live in a house where everyone was exactly alike? (Diversity, Tolerance, Variety) What are the different kinds of chores that the various members of your family perform? What happens when one of you doesn't do his or her job? (Interdependence, Partnership, Niche)

- Draw a diagram or picture that shows how each member of your family depends on the others family members. (Interdependence, Patterns, Models)

- In what ways do you compete with others in your family? How do you cooperate with them? Which do you do most? What happens when you become too competitive? (Partnership, Diversity, Cause/Effect)

- What happens when a new baby is born into a family? (Co-creation, Diversity, Interdependence, Partnership).

- How many ways do you use to communicate with others? (Energy Flow, Information Flow, Feedback Cycles)

- How is your family different now than it was a year ago? Five years ago? What do you think it will be like when you are 10? Why? (Change, Diversity, Adaptation)

- What are the rules that determine how you spend your money? What would your family do with more money? With less money? (Sustainability, Limits)

- How would your life be different if you lived in your neighbor's house instead of your own? If you lived in the next block, or a different city. (Habitat) How do you get along with your neighbors? How are your neighbors like you, and how are they different from you? (Community, Diversity)

Focus Question: What Is Culture?

- What kinds of resources does a neighborhood, town, city, and country need? How does its resources influence a town or a nation? What happens when a neighborhood, town, city, or country uses up all its resources? What can you know about a culture from its location? (Sustainability, Carrying Capacity, Habitat, Niche)

- How do people in a culture communicate with each other? (Energy Flow, Feedback Cycles, Information Flow, Patterns)

- How do cultures change over time? (Change, Stability, Diversity)

- Why are cultures different from each other? (Diversity, Adaptation, Change, Choice, Values) How do people in a culture compete with each other? How do they cooperate? (Partnership) Suppose all cultures were exactly alike? (Diversity, Partnership, Tolerance)

- How do the forms of transportation (or tools or food or shelter or technology) in a culture reflect the needs of the people? (Adaptation, Structure/Function, Creativity, Cause/Effect, Probability/Prediction)

- What kinds of rules do cultures need? (Limits) How are decisions made concerning rules? (Choice, Diversity, Cooperation/Competition)

Focus Question: What Does it Mean to be Human?

- In what ways is diversity built into our bodies? How are our bodies like systems? How are our minds like systems? How do the cells in our bodies compete/cooperate?

- How is my body like the Earth, like the Milky Way Galaxy, like a pond, like an earthworm?

- In what ways is my body a community or neighborhood?

- What kinds of energy does my body require to be healthy? What kinds of energy do I put into my body?

- How is language a feedback loop? How are my emotions a feedback loop? What kind of feedback do my various emotions give me? How are my thoughts a feedback loop? How can I learn from these feedback loops?

- How many different roles do I play each day? In what ways are these roles similar or different? Which is the real "me"?

- What kinds of limits/rules do I live by? What happens when I ignore these limits or break these rules? Which ones can I ignore without negative consequences?

- What cycles and patterns shape my life? What can I learn about myself from them?

- In what kinds of situations am I most creative, least creative?

Focus Question: How Does One Live Responsibly in the Global Community?

- What is the relationship between global resource distribution and national stability and global stability? What is meant by "bio-regionalism"? What would bio-regionalism do to local economies, to national economies, to global economies?

- What forms of communication are best suited to enhance global cooperation?

- What features do all cultures share? Which are distinctively different? What have we to learn from other cultures? What does our culture have to teach other cultures? Who decides which things are good and which things are bad about another culture? about your own culture? What is meant by "cultural hypnosis"?

- What is a reasonable standard of living for all humans based on the available resources? What changes would have to occur if everyone was to have "enough"?

- What is the carrying capacity of Planet Earth? How does technology affect the carrying capacity? What determines the carrying capacity of the planet, or a nation, or a region?

- How has technology decreased sustainability? How can technology improve sustainability?

- How can we learn from "patterns of change"?

- In what areas is it healthy to compete and in what areas is it more healthy to cooperate?

- How can we increase the number of self-governing communities without causing anarchy?

- What are the macro-constraints within which human societies must learn to live?

- What kinds of rules would be necessary to live cooperatively in the global village? What kinds of rules govern other villages?

Introducing Concepts in the Classroom

I have found that one of the best ways to introduce concepts is "clustering," a form of concept mapping that Gabrielle Rico uses as a brainstorming strategy for creative writing. It is a simple and extremely useful technique for creating a collective cognitive map, sometimes called a mind map or a concept map. The process is simple: The teacher puts the concept on the board or on a sheet of newsprint, draws a circle around it, and invites students to brainstorm any words that come into their minds. The words are added to the map either arbitrarily or by connecting each new word to one already on the board. The only rule is that *anything goes.* The teacher must avoid the temptation to edit the contributions of the students. Comments like, "How does that fit?" or "Are you sure that's what you mean?" send messages that soon discourage anyone from participating. This is not the time for discussion or detailed explanations. These can come later. It is appropriate and often helpful for the teacher to add words that he or she thinks might help students understand or use the concept. Figure 6-3 is a clustered concept map created by a sixth grade class as an introduction to a discussion about global cooperation.

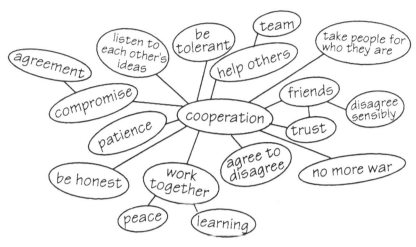

Figure 6-3. Clustering the Concept "Cooperation"

In addition to introducing new ideas and concepts to students, clustering provides the teacher with useful information. For example, it is a great way to discover misconceptions or lack of understanding such as those that often occur in math. For example, a second grade teacher whose children were having difficulty with simple addition and subtraction problems decided to cluster the two concepts, *addition and subtraction*. She found to her surprise, that more than half her students didn't understand what the concepts meant. When she acknowledged in my workshop that "of course, they understand 'more than' and 'less than,'" I suggested that the problem was a language problem not a conceptual problem. Once her students understood that addition always meant "more than," and subtraction always meant "less than," their math scores improved almost overnight. A fifth grade teacher couldn't seem to make her students learn about fractions until she first associated "fraction" with "a part of." I would venture to suggest most of the difficulty students have with math would be eliminated if teachers learned ways to introduce math principles and concepts in simple, understandable ways before moving on to "math facts."

In another workshop, I suggested to a high school math teacher whose inner-city students couldn't understand how to find the area of a triangle, that he try clustering the concept of *area*. He found that while all of his student understood what the concept, *area,* meant, e.g., *turf,* only a few had associated *what they already knew* with the formal mathematical definition that he had been using in class. Thereafter, when he asked students to determine the "turf of a triangle," almost everyone got it right. They knew the correct formula. They just couldn't conceptualize what he was asking them to do. Once he was certain they understood the concept, he reintroduced the formal definition and demonstrated how it was related to their own experience of "area."

Clustering also helps teachers find out what students already know. I have had many teachers share their surprise to find that almost without exception, whenever they introduced a new concept one or more of the students *already understood it.* Based on the clues that other students gain from those who already know it, the students often learn the concept without additional help from the teacher. Following a clustering session, I have found it useful to have the class, either collectively or in cooperative teams, create their own shared definition of the concept. If these definitions need expanding, as with a more formal definition, the teacher can add whatever is necessary to insure that students have fully grasped the relevant implications of the concept.

Since math is often the most difficult subject to incorporate into an integrated curriculum, Donna Stockman's seventh grade team decided to design an integrated unit around three concepts that were being taught in math — reasoning, problem-solving, and communication. In the process, students learned that these concepts are relevant to more than just math and that different subjects — science, social studies, literature, and art — provide a different perspective on each of the concepts. In addition, students learned that just as various subjects have different content, they also have distinctive, though similar, processes.

Concept mapping is also a powerful strategy for helping students understand the relationships that exist among concepts. Joseph Novak and D. Bob Gowin (1984) provide an excellent discussion of concepts and their role in learning as well as a series of suggestions about how to introduce concept mapping at the various grade levels. As with clustering, concept maps help teachers see how students conceptualize the relationships among the various concepts being studied. Seldom, if ever, are two concept maps exactly alike, and students can learn from each other by comparing and contrasting their mental models. While there is no such thing as a "wrong" concept map, teachers can often tell when a student is confused about the meaning of a particular concept. Concept maps become marvelous crib sheets for remembering detailed information. After one high school biology teacher taught his students how to make concept maps, they created a huge room-length concept map on a chalkboard. Throughout the year, as new concepts were introduced, they were added to the map. This map became a powerful shared cognitive organizer for everyone in the class and often engendered in-depth discussions about the relationships among the concepts. Figure 6-4 is a concept map for the integrated unit "What does it mean to be human?"

Perhaps the most effective way to introduce these concepts is to have students "discover" them by studying natural communities. There are a

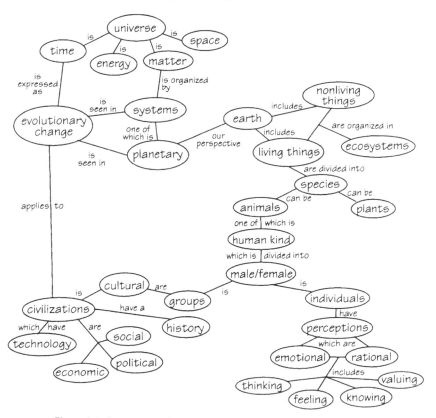

Figure 6-4. Concept Map for Unit on "What Does It Mean to be Human?"

variety of very powerful hands-on activities that provide an experiential introduction to some of these ecological principles. One of the best resources for such activities is Steve Van Matre (1972, 1974). His Institute for Earth Education has developed a series of highly imaginative experiental activities and programs designed to teach many of the same concepts discussed here. At Thompson, teams have often begun the year with field trips to a nearby prairie, a farm, or to the Fox River, which runs through St. Charles. The sixth grade students also participate in outdoor education programs, which are ideal opportunities for students to gain some in-depth understanding of these concepts. For example, Ruth Ann Dunton's team designed a program where students explored five different ecosystems — prairie, pond, marsh, deciduous forest, and pine forest — using the same systems concepts discussed above. Because these principles had been used to frame their studies since the beginning of the semester, students were familiar with them and were able to apply them in a natural setting with ease. Later, in the spring, the students conducted a river study, which allowed them to explore the Fox River from the same perspectives.

Two of the eighth grade teams used a visit to the restored prairie at nearby Fermilab as the basis for an integrated science unit using the concepts of diversity, change, and structure/function. The purpose of the trip was

> NOT for students to memorize specific facts but instead to internalize the "feel," the "look," the "smell," and the "sounds," of the prairie.... It was exciting to see students of all ability levels apply knowledge and skills learned in the science classroom to the activities they participated in on the field trip — and then to see them bring their field trip experiences into other academic classrooms, e.g., using a prairie background for a play being performed in Language Arts. It was obvious that they had experienced the real thing. The questions generated by our study of the prairie ecosystem were investigated throughout the year and served as sources of additional questions on many different topics.

Conclusion

Given the centrality of concepts in thinking and learning, it is surprising to find that few teachers have any idea of how knowledge is structured or the role that concepts play in thinking and learning as we interpret and make meaning from our experiences of the world. Their ignorance is illustrated by the sixth grade teacher who, in a workshop, shared her concern that students couldn't remember how to do math word problems from one day to the next. They could do them on Friday, but by Monday had apparently forgotten the process. I suggested that they had a problem with concept development. Obviously surprised at my suggestion, after giving it some thought, she agreed. Her response was: What can I do about it?

I have found that once teachers understand how concepts can be used in curriculum design and are then introduced to the ecological concepts, they have no difficulty in identifying relevant applications in their own subject areas. For example, when I first introduced the ecological concepts discussed above to the Thompson teachers, I assigned each faculty team one of the concepts that was written on a sheet of newsprint. Then, with a teacher on each side using a different color magic marker, they brainstormed all of the connections they could think of in their particular subject. After a few minutes, they rotated and, after reading what had been written by the other teacher, repeated the process. They continued the process until everyone had written on all four sides. The result was a colorful collage of ideas all of which, in one way or another, related to the original concept. Not only had each team created a resource for curriculum planning that could be used in the coming months, they had also learned a strategy that could be used in the future both among themselves and with students.

On another occasion, I had the opportunity to work with the St. Charles High School department chairpersons to identify a short list of concepts that could be used as a "vertical framework" by teachers in all disciplines at all grade levels. I asked each participant to list the five concepts they considered to be essential to an understanding of their disciplines. The three that appeared most often were *interdependence, diversity,* and *structure/function. Systems* and *change* were also included in several lists. The process that I began with the department chairs was later expanded to involve other members of the district-wide curriculum committee, which included teachers and administrators from the various levels. A few months later the committee finalized a list of eight concepts that could be used as integrative principles both horizontally across disciplinary boundaries and vertically across grade levels. The eight concepts are:

systems, diversity, structure/function, change, balance, sustainability, interdependence, and valuing.

While these concepts have no formal status within the district, they
are being used informally. For example, seventh grade social studies teacher
Dan Kroll decided to design an entire unit around the concept of *values* and
valuing. One of the unique features of this unit was the flexible schedule
agreed upon by the team. Dan had the students for five consecutive periods
a day for a full week. This provides an exciting opportunity for continuity
and intensive participation, with some team work and some individual
work. When the week was over, students expressed appreciation for the
opportunity to study something without the normal interruption that
meant starting all over again each day.

Dan first had students brainstorm a list of current social problems,
e.g., environmental damage, homelessness, hunger, crime, violence, and
intolerance. This was followed by a discussion of the values that seemed to
control the thinking and action which led to these problems, e.g., right and
wrong, responsibility, power, greed, sportsmanship, and innocent until
proven guilty. Each day students clipped articles from the *Chicago Tribune*
and placed these in personal portfolios along with a brief written summary
of each issue and related values. The final product was a poster collage
reflecting a value message that the student wished to convey with the
poster. One girl created a poster on political leadership. She collected
pictures of all the world's political leaders she could find and identified
them by name and country. Across the poster in bold letters was the slogan,
"Would you buy a used car from these guys?" The poster's effectiveness
was demonstrated by a lengthy all-class discussion about political leadership in general and some of the world's leaders in particular. In a roundtable
discussion at the end of the unit, Kroll found that "students could not
believe they talked at home during dinner about the daily news. Even
parents were surprised at their comments and maturity on these social
issues." Needless to say, students have a much more complete understanding of *values* and *valuing* as a result of the unit.

Whether discussed individually or as a group, because of their universal relevance, these ecological concepts provide a powerful conceptual
framework that encompasses all disciplines and all knowledge. Whether

one is learning previously constructed knowledge or constructing new knowledge from bits of information, this framework can become an indispensable aid for lifelong learning.

Chapter Seven

Implementing an
Integrated Curriculum

Twenty-eight children represent 28 little dramas exploding around us at every moment. One of the first tasks of education is to return man to himself ... to help people become truly responsive and therefore truly responsible. (George Leonard)

The implementation of new ideas and strategies is not easy and does not occur overnight. Thompson seventh grade team leader Donna Stockman wrote, early in the first year:

The primary impact of these sessions is that we are questioning everything in our curriculum. There is some dissatisfaction with the thought that most of what we hold near and dear is on its way out — a hard pill to swallow — due to the changing view of the curriculum. I still have a real block on how things will look. Can we ease into these significant alternations? HELP!

I remember the first coaching session Kurt and I had with Donna's team. Their agenda focused on how the team members could juggle the individual curriculum units they were planning to teach so there could be some semblance of integration. For example, they struggled to rearrange their schedules so Bob's Biome unit might coincide with Dan's unit on European history. Donna tried to reschedule her unit on the novel in order to include novels that might be appropriate to the other units. The entire morning was spent trying to fit the units — like a jigsaw puzzle — into what was essentially an interdisciplinary rather than an integrated curriculum.

By the end of the second year, things were different. During the last coaching session of the year the team planned an integrated unit based on the three math "processes/concepts" — reasoning, problem-solving, and communication — discussed in Chapter Six. The difference between this session and the first one was so obvious that I could not resist reminding them of that earlier session more than two years before and noting how far they have traveled in the interim. After two years Donna reflects:

> There was the notion that this integrated curriculum was just like so many other short-lived educational buzz words. But this, it seems, has turned out to be different. Once you become a convert, there's no real turning back. Becoming a convert, however, is at best a very personal struggle and at worst a knockdown, drag-out fight with your colleagues.

Donna is now one of the most enthusiastic supporters of the shifts that have taken place. A wise leader, Donna has kept the team moving slowly but surely, and every session has included at least one excited report on something new that had worked. And yet, it isn't always easy. Well into her third year working with the integrated curriculum — now with two new team members — she describes the process as "two steps forward and one step back."

For many teams, the first step was to design an interdisciplinary unit. Seventh grade reading teacher Peg Anderson had attended a series of my "Environmentalizing Your Teaching" workshops several years earlier and had been making efforts to integrate her material with other members of her team for some time. Since she had spent several years in Japan, she encouraged the social studies teacher to include a study of Japan in his survey of world cultures. She then reinforced that study with stories about Japan and Japanese culture.

The Process of Change

Transformative change is a long-term, systemic process that moves through rather clearly defined stages (Maver 1991). However, because

external change always reflects some internal transformative experience —
a true "a ha!" insight — its twists and turns are seldom predictable. This
means that you always have to begin where people are in the process. By
understanding these stages, one is better able to identify both individual
and group needs more accurately and then respond to those needs creatively. Because each of these stages involves a genuine shift in consciousness, these shifts cannot be rushed. Change is a process that goes from
unawareness to *awareness* to *understanding* to *(re)visioning* to *commitment.*

Unawareness

A person who is unaware of any need for change is, to use psychologist Charles Tart's term, "asleep" (Tart 1987). Many teachers — and administrators — today seem to be asleep. They go through life making all of the
day-by-day decisions that are required of them — grades, attendance records, teaching plans — without ever thinking seriously about or reflecting
on what they are doing. These people are satisfied to let someone else make
the important policy decisions concerning the curriculum, learning outcomes, and grading policies. Although they may be vaguely aware that
serious problems exist, they assume there is nothing they can do to make a
difference, so they simply ignore them. Suggested changes like major
curriculum reform are viewed at best with skepticism and often with
disdain.

Awareness

Charles Tart refers to the second stage as "waking up." It is as if, like
Rip Van Winkle, one literally wakes up from a long sleep. At first there is a
dawning realization that you have been asleep. Then you look around and
suddenly see things with new eyes. One Thompson teacher put it succinctly.
"You can't change the world in a day, but the world can change in a second!"

The awareness stage in the change process occurs when people recognize that before they can address the serious problems that exist, they
need to gain some perspective on the situation. These people are ready to
move into the next stage of the change process.

Although he had taken a Cooperative Learning workshop, Bill was in
his last year of teaching and reluctant to make any changes. He recalls the

experience:

> Knowing what kind of group I was getting, I decided to go to straight rows, lectures, homework problems, etc. I wore myself out trying to answer all of the questions, discipline was worse; it just wasn't fun. After three days I decided to try some cooperative learning structures. Wow, what a difference! We started to enjoy the class, kids began to participate, discipline improved immensely. It's amazing the difference from the "old" ways of teaching.

Understanding

Understanding — true comprehension — requires two things: thoughtfulness (what physicist Peter Russell calls "self-reflective consciousness") and context (the big picture). Once one perceives education from this broader perspective, it becomes clear that the many seemingly separate, unsolvable problems are really symptoms of a single, more basic structural problem. For example, from this perspective it becomes clear that all of the problems identified in *A Nation At Risk* and the other national reports, such as the 23 million who are functionally illiterate adults, are merely symptoms of a deep and profound systemic design problem. This insight is like finally recognizing, as one person put it, that your balloon is covered with patches and it's time to get a new balloon.

Ruth Ann Dunton returned to teaching after 14 years with some understandable anxiety but knowing that she "wanted to be a part of re-defining education because it had been apparent to me in those earlier years that something was wrong with the way we were doing things." She quickly found that the "camaraderie of five teachers sharing the same students and philosophy" and the student-centered approach at Thompson was exactly what she had been looking for. She reflects, "as a professional I am beginning to see the bigger picture of how all of the parts fit together — the connectedness, the contextual questions, the concepts, the content areas, the process skills, the District 303 Outcomes, the assessment, and the many courses I have taken." Three years later, now as team leader, Ruth Ann wrote, "I'll probably always be growing, changing, looking for answers, moving along in search of the big picture — just as I hope my students are."

(Re)visioning, Commitment, and Action

Once you've gotten your bearings and understand the nature of the dilemma, you are ready to create what Paul Hawken calls a "vision of potential." What would my classroom look like if every student was really a potential genius? What would a curriculum that addressed students' real questions look like? Suppose I could teach the way I always wanted to teach? As that vision becomes clear and you see what really may be possible, you are ready to make a commitment to do whatever is necessary to make that vision a reality. Such a commitment, in turn, energizes both individual and collective action. Action, once begun, in turn engenders a new and more encompassing vision of other possibilities — "Now that I've made this change, perhaps I can try something even more daring!" This is followed by a new level of commitment and even more energized action. In the words of one Thompson teacher, "I learned to take little steps. Little by little they got bigger."

Kurt Anderson describes this process as "struggling to identify our own core values." In his words,

> As we have confronted the issues of student-centered learning by focusing on their questions rather than our answers, we have found ourselves struggling to identify our own core values — the real reasons that we entered the teaching profession. We began to recognize that this was the type of education that each one of us truly believed in but never had the opportunity to deliver. Now, as we are attempting to transform our teaching from a content-driven to a student-initiated curriculum, we are finding that it is our own internal value structures which keep us going. The frustration and excitement of our work is that we are both discovering and creating the future at the same time! Because we truly believe that what we are doing is best for the kids, we are finding ways to remove the barriers that stand between us and actualizing our vision. At Thompson, because of the mutual support derived from the energy, excitement, and tenacity of the staff, the hard work of eliminating barriers is going on day after day.

This struggle is often quite messy — and scary. As team leader Chuck Robinson put it, "We're all taking risks — not teaching what we are 'supposed to teach.'" On the other hand, when one persists as Bonnie has done, it's like "coming to the end of a very long tunnel and suddenly seeing light." The rewards come with the new insights. Kurt Anderson records one of his "a ha!" insights. "I suddenly realized that it wasn't the curriculum we were trying to integrate. We are trying to integrate learning." And, he continues, "it is happening."

> Teachers are identifying only the parameters of the topics and letting students wrestle with outcomes. Teachers and students are learning together as teachers learn to become facilitators. Peers are meeting to talk about the art and science of teaching and viewing "content" with a critical eye and asking "Is this really important for all kids to know?" The LRC Director is pulling her hair out because, all of a sudden, more information on more things in more depth is needed each day. Students are becoming invested in their education as they investigate issues that are meaningful to them. Yes, we have begun to integrate the curriculum — and learning — throughout the entire school.

Implementing Change at the District Level

St. Charles District 303 has made an administrative commitment to substantive change, which has involved several simultaneous, long-term processes. Recognizing that such change had to begin with teachers, a decision was made to offer a wide variety of staff development programs. While attendance was always optional, to encourage their involvement, teachers received either a per diem remuneration or credit toward salary increments for participation. Early on, workshops in Process Writing and Whole Language were highly popular among elementary and middle school Language Arts teachers — and resulted in the implementation of these two learner-centered, contextual strategies in most elementary schools and in the Language Arts programs at Thompson.

This was followed by a variety of special programs for gifted students. With substantial Federal funding, the gifted programs provided new opportunities to help students learn and led to a variety of new teaching strategies, many of which were student-centered and called for a different role for the teacher.

Because these programs and strategies were both effective and more satisfying for teachers and students, teachers began to ask, "If these programs work for the gifted kid, why won't they work for everyone?" In short, the gifted program provided the context for making a major conceptual leap — in Kurt Anderson's words, "the gifted aren't the only ones who can learn." In time this led to what Kurt calls "detracking." Today, with the exception of an accelerated math program and a few students assigned to special education, all children are placed in heterogeneous groups. And, due to the new inclusion program, special education students at Thompson are fully participating members of the regular science, social studies, and language arts classes.

In 1990, the St. Charles School Board initiated a formal process to create a district-wide strategic plan that would involve groups of parents, teachers, community members, and students. Working in teams for more than a year, these people wrote a districtwide plan that included the following mission statement.

The mission of the St. Charles School District is to educate students who will:

- think critically,
- communicate effectively,
- value and demonstrate high ethical conduct,
- possess positive self-esteem,
- contribute to their community, and
- excel among people throughout the world

by providing a vigorous and dynamic educational system characterized by:

- a caring, dedicated and highly competent staff,
- innovative instruction,
- emerging technology, and
- comprehensive programs

in partnership with an involved and supportive community.

In September 1991, a Curriculum Steering Committee was formed to develop a philosophy and broad curriculum statement for each subject area that reflected the new district mission statement. Over a two-year period, this group with the support of a community-based Curriculum Advisory Council, consisting of parents, teachers, students, and business leaders, developed a vision of the "Graduate of the year 2000." The decision was made to emphasize what skills and abilities the St. Charles High School graduate should possess, rather than the more traditional listing of courses required for graduation. Heavily influenced by the studies done at Alverno College in Milwaukee, in 1992 the district officially adopted the following seven "exit outcomes."

Students shall be able to demonstrate what it means to . . .

- Communicate effectively

- Think critically
- Exhibit creativity
- Display interpersonal skills, self-understanding, and ethical conduct
- Demonstrate global responsibility and cross-cultural understanding
- Develop and maintain personal wellness practices
- Access and use information effectively

These exit outcomes are our most distant instructional targets, telling in broad terms what we expect students to know and be able to do when they complete twelve years of schooling.

Students achieving these outcomes will become life-long learners. This life-long learning may include college, technical and other formal post-secondary learning as well as informal, personalized learning. These students will be prepared to meet the challenges of career decision making and employment responsibilities.

In 1992 the Curriculum Steering Committee recognized the need for content outcomes to complement the process outcomes listed above. The decision was made to identify several fundamental concepts and principles that were common to all subjects, and which students needed to grasp before graduating from high school. Using a participatory process referred to in Chapter Six, the Committee identified eight concepts that graduates of St. Charles High School would be expected to understand and apply in the context of the various academic disciplines. These concepts are: *systems, diversity, structure/function, change, balance, sustainability, interdependence and valuing.* Although these concepts have not been officially adopted by the School Board, they are used as curriculum organizing principles by the Thompson faculty.

Implementing Change at the School Level

In response to the districtwide mission, in the spring of 1991, Kurt Anderson invited the faculty and staff of Thompson Middle School to collectively create a mission statement that was appropriate for their school. He describes the visioning process that he used with the teachers:

I asked them to imagine themselves walking into and through the school building while visualizing what would for them be the "ideal" setting. I tried to focus their thinking with questions like: What is happening? What are the kids doing? What are teachers doing? What do the classrooms look like? Finally, I had them exit the building and

walk out to the street and then look back. Then I asked them to envision
a large marquee in front of the building with a single word on it — one
which capsulized what was happening inside. We then collected these
words and used them to create the following mission statement.

Thompson Middle School is committed to nurturing and involving students and adults in an environment which emphasizes cooperation,
discovery, and enjoyment.

Our school community strives to develop responsible citizens who possess positive self-esteem, respect for others, and interest in lifelong learning.

In June 1993, Thompson Middle School was selected as the site for a
pilot project to "integrate the curriculum around the outcomes" and I was
invited to be the curriculum consultant. In the initial curriculum integration
workshop the district exit outcomes" became a focal point for curriculum
design. Unlike behavioral objectives, which had dominated a generation of
educational thinking, these outcomes provided a direction without defining a specific route. Because they were based on a vision of potential that
combined both idealism and realism, they provided an ideal starting point
for designing an integrated curriculum.

In addition to the district outcomes, teachers were asked to generate
a second set of outcomes that reflected the real-life questions which their
students were asking. After a great deal of discussion, they agreed that the
seven questions identified at the beginning of Chapter Five were repre-
sentative of student concerns, e.g., "How do I relate to my peers?" Given
these two sets of outcomes, it immediately became evident that very little
of the present curriculum content was appropriate to either. As teachers
then began to identify their own personal learning outcomes for the workshop it was clear that most of them both recognized the need for substantive
changes in the curriculum and were open to it. In terms of the schema above,
they were "awake." They were open to new ideas and insights that would
help them better understand both the need for change and ways they could
creatively and imaginatively respond to that need. At this point I shared
my own anticipated outcome for the workshop: Using the contextual
strategies that would be introduced in the workshop — discussed in Chapters Four, Five, and Six — each team would complete the outline of an
integrated curriculum that addressed the three sets of outcomes — district,
student, and personal — discussed above.

The initial workshop was only a beginning. Of equal importance were the follow-up support strategies that Kurt Anderson recognized were necessary if the teachers were to have a relatively non-threatening environment in which they could take risks and try new ideas. The most significant of these strategies has been a series of team-oriented coaching sessions that Kurt and I conducted. In these sessions, the team was expected to set its own agenda — sometimes a difficult and uncomfortable experience particularly with two perceived "experts" sitting at the table. However, as teachers began to understand that they really were able to create their own context for learning, a readiness and openness that had been absent earlier began to emerge. This experience, in and of itself, was a powerful catalyst for change. Kurt reflects on these sessions:

> One of the most significant experiences that we have had during this process of eliminating barriers is our participation in the coaching sessions which Ed and I have conducted with the interdisciplinary teaching teams representing language arts, math, reading, social studies and science. The teams set their own agenda and the two half-day sessions per semester are usually a combination of assessment and planning. Here we experience the push and pull of professionals struggling with their issues in ways that model the process they will be following in the classroom. We learned quite early that the conversations that take place among a multi-disciplinary team are quite different from those that occur when teachers are talking with their counterparts in science, math, or literature. Here we are all "students," asking of each other tough questions like "Why do we need to know that?" or "Do you really need to spend all of that time on dividing fractions?" It is during these sessions that I, as principal, get a more realistic picture of what is going on in the classrooms. Believe me, I now know what is really happening in our building!

Although the teams set their own agendas in these coaching sessions, it was clear from the beginning that the macro-constraints for our discussions were the districtwide outcomes. At Thompson, these are posted on the wall of the conference room where the coaching sessions are held. Whenever the discussion relates to curriculum, the challenge is explicit — which of these outcomes are you working on and how do you see what you are planning contributing to those outcomes?

On some occasions there is still resistance. While this outcome-focused approach to curriculum design seems obvious — "if you don't know where you want to go, any direction will get your there" — experience has demonstrated that when teachers are released from the regimen of textbooks and worksheets, they often tend to design their curriculum around activities that strike their fancy without considering the learning objective. I remember one coaching session that was being directed by the team leader. Resisting any intrusion by Kurt or myself, he began by describing an activity that he thought would provide an interesting multidisciplinary experience for the students. After listening to his description of the activity for a few minutes, Kurt asked: "What are the outcomes you are seeking?" After a few minutes of very general and primarily irrelevant responses, he returned to a discussion of the activity, seeking input from the other members of the team. Once again, Kurt asked his question and received the same response. The team leader continued to ignore the question of outcomes and, to use Sam Keen's (1994) colorful expression, "He jumped on his horse and sped off in all directions." In this case, the horse was an activity dear to the team leader's heart and, because of the team's past history, everyone else was swift to follow him. The irony is that the activity was a good one and could well have been adapted to address important learning outcomes. Unfortunately, two years later the team continues to be activity-centered rather than focused on outcomes.

There is nothing wrong with good activities, most of which can be adapted in one way or another to support desired learning outcomes. However, well-thought-out outcomes can help a team of teachers sharpen the focus of an activity so that its impact is even greater than originally anticipated.

Because of the strong emphasis on outcomes, Kurt has been asked on several occasions by outsiders whether District 303 or Thompson Middle School has adopted Outcome Based Education (OBE). He hastens to answer in the negative and explains that while outcomes play an important role in curriculum design at Thompson Middle School and throughout the district, "We see outcomes as a process and not a program."

The following five questions were found to be helpful in facilitating the redesign of curriculum by teams at Thompson:

1. What are the desired outcomes?

   These do not have to be identified in behavioral terms. It is entirely appropriate that words such as "know, understand, appreciate" be used. It is important, however, to be as specific as possible because in the final analysis, the assessment of an outcome is implicit in the description of the outcome itself. While it is important to identify the more general districtwide outcomes, this question focuses attention on the more specific, existential outcomes related to specific units or activities.

Recognizing that students had to understand the districtwide outcomes and their implications for assessment, eighth grade team leader Chuck Robinson spent a number of class periods having students put the outcomes in their own words. The relevance of these general outcomes became apparent as students applied them to their own learning experiences. For example, when asked to define what it meant to communicate effectively, students decided on the following:

- A right to hear and be heard

- Talk loudly enough to be heard

- Speak clearly

- Make sure people understand what you mean

- Share ideas

- Use appropriate body language

- Use eye contact

- Face person when speaking

- Listen to speaker

- Contribute ideas in discussion and conversation

- Speak with feeling

- Speak when it is appropriate

- Be able to talk in big groups

- Express yourself

- Use appropriate oral and written language

The complete list of student-generated outcomes became a powerful medium that was then used by both teachers and students for assessment purposes. Following Chuck's lead, other teams used similar strategies to make certain that students understood the outcomes and could see their practical relevance to classroom activities. Using their own outcomes as guidelines, students quickly learned the skills of self- and peer-assessment, which, when combined with teacher assessment, provided powerful feedback that enhanced learning in unanticipated ways. It wasn't long before some teams had their students identifying both the anticipated outcomes for a given project and the way they wished to have these outcomes assessed. Another teacher comments that "We discuss outcomes with students a lot; I'll bet 50% of our kids could name our district outcomes better than 80% of our district teachers!!"

2. What knowledge and skills are needed to reach these outcomes?

Teachers are encouraged to identify the conceptual framework, e.g., the concepts and basic ideas, which are relevant to the goals. The skills are often similar to the districtwide learning outcomes, e.g., critical thinking. By selecting only knowledge that is appropriate to the outcomes, a great deal of extraneous information — often the core of traditional curriculum content — is recognized as being irrelevant to the desired outcome and is discarded.

Initially, some teachers had difficulty letting go of their favorite content. One teacher was concerned that she could no longer use her favorite ancedotes and jokes. However, they soon began to realize that they did not always face an either/or option. For example, Janet Fosnot, an eighth grade social studies teacher at Thompson, found that even though she still decided the content topic,

> Students generated their own questions and then we used the cooperative learning strategy of "Jigsaw" to do the learning. I have seldom seen as much excitement and togetherness as I saw when students met in my room at 7:30 a.m. (school starts at 8:30), came in during lunch periods, or met at each others' homes.

3. What is the best way to gain the knowledge and skills?

While occasionally, the decision may be for the teacher to make a formal presentation, for the most part, teachers at Thompson have found interesting and exciting ways to involve students in researching their own questions. For example, a program suitably called "I Search" provides a popular methodology by which students seek answers to their own questions. Through a variety of strategies, students become increasingly involved in a wide variety of problem-solving experiences, or in other creative, practical activities — many of which the students design themselves.

One sixth grade student wrote in her journal, "What I liked about I-search is that it was a ton more fun than research. With I-search you can have fun while doing it. My friend and I even took our I-search to the princable(sic) (Mr. Anderson)."

4. How will everyone know when the outcomes have been achieved?

This is the assessment/feedback step. To understand this step, it is important to recognize that, from a systemic perspective, the primary purpose of assessment is to provide feedback to the learner in a way that enables her to more fully achieve the learning outcome. For example, in his studies of mastery learning, Benjamin Bloom (1984) concludes that, given an appropriate learning environment — *one that includes immediate, accurate, and continuous feedback* in addition to ample time — virtually all students have the potential for achieving above-average grades.

While teachers often feel the need to identify some formal assessment process, increasingly students are encouraged to identify their own presentation and assessment processes. Two useful and important forms of assessment that are used to complement the teacher's assessment are a student's self-assessment and peer assessment. Both of these provide useful feedback to students and have become a common feature for many teams.

Assessment practices at Thompson have changed dramatically in the last few years. Students appreciate the new and different emphasis in evaluation. During a final class assessment, in response to the question, What did you learn about yourself?, one sixth grader wrote, "I learned that I am a good reader." In response to the question, What did you learn about life?, his response was, "There are more questions than answers." Not bad insights for a sixth grader. Another sixth grader wrote, "I like not having tests and quizzes. It is more fun to read for your own enjoyment. I remember more and enjoy it more when I don't have to use the information on a test."

In my workshops, in a kind of "tongue-in-cheek" manner, I add a fifth question to the Curriculum Planning Workshop. Unfortunately, for many, if not most, educators this is still the only question that really counts.

5. How will you prove that the outcomes have been achieved?

This is supposedly the reason for quantification — an attempt to "objectively" prove success! Since District 303 still required grades it is still a necessary step. However, in the context of this systemic rubric, teachers are reminded that grades merely reflect another form of subjective evaluation.

Grades are still an enigma for some teachers. During one coaching session, one team leader described a new and exciting set of activities that he had introduced to his class. Following these activities, he had the students do a self-evaluation by describing in writing what they had learned. This was followed by a verbal peer evaluation by members of the cooperative learning team. Although both of these assessments were useful and effective, he felt the need to also give a traditional 25-item multiple choice test. When he was asked why he had added the test to what already seemed to have been an excellent evaluation process, he said, rather sheepishly, "I wanted to have something to base a grade on."

Doug's initial discomfort in giving a grade that he couldn't substantiate in some "objective" way is shared by many other teachers at Thompson. Their mindset made it difficult to acknowledge that it is just as valid to translate other forms of assessment into a letter grade as it is to write a series of 25 "objective" multiple choice items. However, teachers have become comfortable enough with alternative assessment strategies so that most use a letter grade only at the end of the grading period. All of the teams actively encourage alternative modes of presentation and assessment. Students have written and acted out plays and various other dramatic presentations, written and produced video programs, created and presented a variety of written and oral responses, journals, newspapers and portfolios, created demonstrations and exhibitions, and completed an assortment of projects and investigations. As a part of a study on primitive culture, students on one sixth grade team created masks and sculptures that were both artistically and culturally outstanding. One student investigation into water usage in the school building — referred to in the next chapter — led to the discovery of several leaking pipes and resulted in some major repairs that not only saved water, but gave students a sense of ownership of their building. As a consequence of several workshops on authentic assessment, all of the teams are now employing a wide variety of alternative assessment rubrics and one team has requested and received permission to substitute other forms of assessment for the traditional letter grades.

> One teacher notes,

> Assessment is based on improvement not what others are doing. The major question is "Did you improve?" not "What grade did you get?" Last year giving tests was the main focus of what we did. Testing is no longer the overriding principle of what we do in class; by drawing their own conclusions and concept mapping, students are living the concepts, not just memorizing them. The kids know now that they are here for learning, not grades. If they forget the grades, if they are learning, the grades will come.

It has been interesting to note in our coaching sessions that while teachers are quite comfortable with identifying the outcomes and designing authentic assessment rubrics, they are less comfortable with determining what skills and knowledge are needed to reach goals and how to attain them. These are the points at which the conflicts inherent in the shift to a learner-centered, integrated curriculum are most sharply focused. The need to cover the content is so deeply embedded in the psyche of most teachers that it is exceedingly difficult for them to determine whether a particular content is appropriate for their desired outcomes. In the same way, in spite of all the evidence to the contrary, most teachers still have a kind of gut feeling that the only way they can be certain students learn what they need to know is through some form of presentation by the teacher.

Curriculum Applications

A recent coaching session provided what might be considered an ideal prototype for a curriculum design process. This was a new eighth grade team that had been together for only two months, with little opportunity for cooperative curriculum design. Only two of the five members had been in either of my curriculum workshops. At the onset, the team leader announced that their agenda was to begin planning for an integrated unit on "Explorations" that would focus on the two concepts, *change* and *structure/function*. I suggested that they consider formulating the theme as a question, e.g., "How have explorations changed the world?" Soon we were deep into a very interactive philosophical discussion about issues like the nature of change, how people respond to change, and their own personal reactions to change. After about an hour, I asked, "What is the desired outcome?" Dan suggested one of the eighth grade social studies outcomes — "To understand how change impacts social, political, and economic decisions in our society."

The discussion continued for another hour, moving back and forth from various outcomes to possible focus questions. The team continued this philosophical conversation as it sought to clarify its own understanding of the structure and function of change, e.g., the linear/nonlinear nature of change and the role that choice and necessity play in change. Toward the end of the session, team members began to explore possible assessment strategies while Kurt wrote the ideas on the blackboard as they emerged and erased those that were dropped. It was only in the last 15 minutes that everything seemed to jell. The focus question was "What are the catalysts for change?" The outcome selected was "To understand how change in various areas impact life in our society." They tentatively decided that one of the best ways to determine how well students understood the impact of change would be to have some form of pre- and post-assessment, e.g., to have students write essays on the focus question before and after the study. They also decided that students would be asked to select some medium through which each could demonstrate how change had influenced them personally.

Later, as Kurt and I reflected on the session, we were both aware, once again, of how important philosophical discussions are in curriculum design. At least three-quarters of this coaching session was spent playing with ideas. As Kurt and I began to retrace the movement of ideas, how they were shaped and reshaped, how some were dropped and others modified into totally new ones, I was reminded of Mary Catherine Bateson's (1994) observation that "the excitment of improvisation lies not only in the risk involved but in the new ideas, as heady as adrenaline of performance, that seem to come from nowhere." Then, after two hours of discussion, in a matter of 15 to 20 minutes, everything came together: the outcome, the focus question, the concepts, and the beginning of an assessment strategy. In preparation for their next team meeting, each teacher was going to identify and circulate a list of ways these could be related to his or her subject area. While Kurt and I both recognized that changes would still take place before the unit was finalized, we knew that the general outline was in place and that the planning process had worked — at a personal level, at a team level, and at a curricular level.

This was a significant first step for this team. Although the final unit will be more interdisciplinary than integrated, the experience was genuinely integrative. As the team leader, a veteran of many such sessions, observed to me later, "That was just what we needed — it gave us a chance to experience the kinds of discussions we hope to have with the kids."

The philosophical implications of questions and concepts are not lost on kids. One team leader writes, "We have found connectedness to be the basis of all we are doing. In fact, connectedness is experienced everywhere: teachers with teachers, teachers with kids, kids with other kids, and subject with subject." Sixth grade teacher, Rex Troyer, and special education teacher, Jan Sutfin, recall an experience that occurred shortly after the first summer workshop. In their words,

> Connections are made all the time that cause students to say, "I got it" and "Yes, that makes sense." The how of developing this environment is usually attributed to the personality of the teacher. In our case, the how is attributed to the entire classroom community. It began with a discussion of the statement, "Everything in this world is connected to everything else." Those sixth grade faces looked dumbfounded. The only sound you could hear were the sounds of bodies trying to become invisible. We co-taught the class using the interruptive style of teaching. When one left off, the other would interrupt with a question or a statement that would keep the students thinking and discussing. Rex started the discussion by asking how many had gone with a parent to buy a new car. A majority of students had had that experience. He asked what happened. Students responded with various answers, all of which ended by parents paying money and taking the car home. Then the connections began. We went from the consumer to the retailer, to the finance companies. We went from the product to the manufacturer to the raw materials. We went from the raw materials to the Earth's resources. We went from the depletion of those resources to recycling and back to ourselves being responsible for the care of the earth. We had begun the connection-making. Over the next several weeks, the dumbfounded faces were replaced with eager expressions and waving hands crying to be recognized. Why? Because education was relevant and connected to our students' lives.

One teacher commented on the difference in "the way we look at kids now versus four years ago…. Today they are handling projects which then would have been reserved for AT [Academically Talented] students." Another teacher noted that "only three students out of 125 are chronically choosing to do poor work — far less than in other years." Doug Thompson observed that "the major strength for the kids this year is that we are talking about the same questions and concepts in all of their classes." And finally from Dan Kroll, "The most unlikely kids have learned."

Principal Kurt Anderson is probably the most enthusiastic supporter of the integrated curriculum, perhaps because he gets so much positive feedback. He records two comments which suggest that something unique and different is occurring at Thompson. The first came from a regular substitute teacher who was being interviewed for a full-time position. He had been in a number of schools in the area and had "never experienced anything like Thompson anywhere else." He continued, "Something is different here. Teachers are happy and eager to do their job and kids seem to come into class anxious to learn and willing to meet high expectations…. Am I in a fog or is this really the way it is around here?"

The second comment came from a junior high teacher from a neighboring district. Having heard about the "exciting things that are happening" from one of Thompson's teachers, he decided to spend a day visiting and observing several classrooms. As he left he said to Kurt, "Wow, what a school! I saw things here today that I never thought could be done. The active learning, student-centeredness and genuine fun that both teachers and kids are having is quite impressive. I want you to come and tell my school how to do this."

I have already noted on several occasions the impact of an integrated, learner-centered curriculum on students who have been labeled learning disabled. There is no better example of this impact than the story of Sarah, an eighth grade LD student as told by special ed teacher Jeanne Humke.

> Sarah began eighth grade saying "I hate school," "I hate science," "I hate writing," etc. Whenever she was given an academic task the word *hate* came out. I think what she was saying was, "I'm unsure of myself and afraid I'll fail." My plan to build her confidence was to help her get caught up in the excitement of learning.

> Sarah did very well in the collaboratively taught science class — particu-

larly in the hands-on lab work. Being a social person she worked well with other students. She began to see connections and experience success. We knew she had made the major change in attitude when we gave the students a cooperative quiz in their groups of four and Sarah spent the entire time kneeling on her chair leaning over the desk so that she was right in the middle of the group giving her input along with the others. We also noticed that she smiled a lot.

In language arts, the students were asked to pick topics that they wished to research. Sarah choose teenage pregnancy. Her sister had her first baby at 15 and was expecting the second at 19. We helped Sarah find materials in the library and she became so absorbed in reading and writing in class that she was oblivious to everything else in the classroom. She wrote a well-thought-out four page typed essay, a letter to her sister's obstetrician, a poem expressing the fears a young teenage mother might have, and a poster with an oral presentation. Because she thought she would be embarrassed presenting the material directly, I videotaped her presentation and we played it to the class.

What was most important for Sarah was not that she had done well in class but that she had found answers that were important for her. In her conclusion she states, "Abstinence is the only way to keep from getting pregnant. No other birth control method will work 100% of the time. When you have a baby, you have to grow up and become an adult. I don't want to do that yet. I still want to be a kid."

As the year ended, Sarah quit using the word "hate," she smiled a lot, was able to accept verbal praise without making a negative comment, and was taking pride in the fact that all of her work was completed.

Conclusion

The important feature of the change model discussed above is that it provides insight as to where people are and what kind of strategies are needed to effect change. For example, if we consider the spectrum of educators — from unaware to committed — on a bell curve we would find that possibly 10 to 20% are sound asleep, while another 10 to 20% are committed to some form of substantive change. This leaves the vast majority, perhaps 60 or 70%, of people in the "waking up" or "aware" category. Too often the tendency of those who are already awake and committed is to focus their attention on those who either are still asleep or have just woken up and are making the most noise, e.g., the radicals on either end of the political spectrum. Unfortunately, it will take the proverbial "2x4 to the head" to even get their attention much less influence the way they think. But I suspect that the vast majority of teachers are looking for something to help them understand what's happening. These people are often those "who know but don't know they know." They are looking for different ways of doing things that makes sense. My experience suggests that many of them are ready for the proposition that everything is connected to everything else. After all, the image of the Earth from space carries a message that thoughtful people will ponder. By challenging them to question tacitly held assumptions about the nature of the world, we encourage the kind of understanding that makes genuine transformation possible. To me this is where the great challenge lies — helping those who are waking up to gain the kind of "big picture" perspective that will enable them to understand the connectedness of things and the responsibility to personal and social transformation that flows from this insight.

Chapter Eight

Designing Schools as Learning Communities

I am dubious as to how far we can move toward global community — which is the only way to achieve international peace — until we learn the basic principles of community in our own individual lives and personal spheres of influence. (Scott Peck 1987)

In response to what he calls the "rampant cult of individualism" that has swept America during the last 50 years and is rapidly "spreading like a cancer around the world," historian Christopher Lasch (1995) notes that "self-governing communities, not individuals (have been) the basic unit of democratic society." He points out that it has always been this local, self-governing community that furnished "the sources of social cohesion" which made life satisfying and meaningful for its members. Here people experienced the "shared assumptions ingrained in folkways, customs, prejudices, habits of the heart" that provided them with both an individual identity and a sense of belonging. In addition to its impact upon its members, the self-governing community promoted and sustained the common good by protecting both the people and their natural resources against outside exploitation. Because of the breakdown of this fundamental social unit, Lasch argues that "a public philosophy for the twenty-first century will have to give more weight to the community than to the right of private decision. It will have to emphasize responsibilities rather than rights."

Since the beginning of human experience, local communities — clans, tribes, villages — have always held a pivotal position as the mediator between the individual and the larger, impersonal outside world. Because political and economic forces outside the community have always tended to be exploitative, without the strength, support, and cohesion of a local community of people, their natural resources rapidly disappear while individuals simultaneously feel increasingly disempowered and disenfranchised.

Today, without the mediating role of a local, self-governing community, the individual is cast adrift, alone in a vast sea of people, isolated from everyone else and dominated by powerful, anonymous forces such as big government and/or large corporations. As is increasingly evident in the political arena, when these two powerful forces combine their strength to mastermind the decisions that shape the lives of everyone in the society, individuals have little more than a token voice. Not only is the individual at the mercy of these impersonal economic and political forces, the natural resources that belong to us all — what ecologist Garrett Hardin calls "the commons" — the air, water, and land upon which all humans depend for survival, are increasingly exploited, often beyond any hope of recovery.

This would suggest, that of the eight global dilemmas identified in Chapter One, the most pivotal and far reaching has been the breakdown of these local, self-governing communities. On the one hand, it has had disastrous consequences for whole societies that have taken the forms of genocide, abject poverty, and ecological devastation, to list but a few. On the other, the loss of supportive communities has resulted in a pervasive sense of helplessness in the face of these disasters on the part of ordinary citizens.

Nowhere is the emphasis on individualism at the expense of community more evident than in the way we educate our children. It should come as no surprise to find that

> The schools ... play a more powerful role in stressing an individual rather
> than a common vision. ... Individual success and achievement are greatly
> emphasized. ... We are taught mostly to learn to be alone, to compete, to

achieve, to succeed.... It is not that the schools, like the culture, are not mindful of social identity, but they clearly put much more emphasis on our personal identity, especially as it relates to our obsession with personal success and achievement. (Purpel 1989)

Not only are we not surprised by the above description, but most adults would probably agree that this is the way it ought to be. I am certain that if asked, the majority of parents would strongly support the current emphasis on competitive achievement and individual success as preparation for the real world. In spite of overwhelming evidence to the contrary (Johnson et al. 1984; Kohn 1986), there is the implicit assumption throughout Western society that competition to promote individual achievement, whether in sports or in school, brings out the best in people. And so, in virtually every facet of the educational experience, children are encouraged to compete with each other — for grades, for class ranking, and for special opportunities such as gifted and college preparatory programs. Two obvious consequences of this focus on competitive striving and individual accomplishment are (a) that while there are a few winners, the great majority of our children are losers, and (b) there is a loss of social cohesion derived from the shared goals and values of community.

As would be expected, this emphasis on the individual at the expense of community gets played out in the larger social arena. In a 1989 survey (Etzioni 1993) high school students were asked what was special about the United States. The two most frequent responses were "Individualism and the fact that it is a democracy and you can do whatever you want" and "We don't have any limits."

This leads me to suggest that the most fundamental social issue confronting Western culture in general and American culture in particular is learning to find a balance between *the rights and the good* of the individual and those of the society as a whole. At its root, this is a philosophical issue — perhaps *the pivotal* philosophical issue facing our nation and humankind today. From this point of view, a primary culprit is our propensity for either/or thinking. An inheritance of Cartesian dualism, this reductionist view of the world incorrectly assumes that the individual and the community represent opposite ends of a continuum of rights and power that exist in a constant win/lose struggle for dominance. The alternative way of visualizing reality, which I have called systems thinking, implicitly recognizes that the common good and the good of the individual are inextricably bound together so that the well-being of either is dependent upon the well-being of the other.

Once we have reconceptualized this dilemma, we will have moved a long way toward resolving the related problems. While I believe that many of us intuitively understand the nature of this apparent impasse, few have conceptualized it in a way that empowers them to change their way of thinking and acting. As sociologist Jane Jacobs (1992) points out, "many of us have taken on casts of mind so skewed toward one set of ... values that we have little understanding of the other, and little if any appreciation of its integrity too."

Cultural tradition to the contrary, it was not always this way. Recognizing that it does indeed take a village to raise a child, the indigenous model described by Tewe Pueblo educator Dr. Gregory Cajete (1994) stands in sharp contrast to the culturally dominant model described above.

> The ideal purpose of education is to attain knowledge, seek truth, wisdom, completeness, and life as perceived by traditional philosophies and cultures around the world.... It embodies a quest for self, individual and community survival, and wholeness in the context of a community and natural environment... The living place, the learner's extended family, the clan and the tribe provided the context and the source for teaching. In this way every situation provided a potential opportunity for learning, and basic education was not separated from the natural, social, or spiritual aspects of everyday life. Living and learning were fully integrated ... (and) unfolded through mutual, reciprocal relationships between one's social group and the natural world. This relationship involved all dimensions of one's being, while providing both personal development and technical skills through *participation* in community life. It was essentially a communally integrated expression of environmental education.

> *Mitakuye Oyasin* (We are all related) is a Lakota phrase that captures an essence of Tribal education because it reflects the understanding that our lives are truly and profoundly connected to other people and the physical world.... Education is, at its essence, learning about life through participation and relationship in community including not only people, but plants, animals, and the whole of Nature. (Cajete 1994)

Since it is primarily the students' future that is at stake, if they are to ever achieve global community, it seems appropriate that schools become the training ground where students learn to work cooperatively in "learning communities." Here they can experience and acquire the insight, knowledge, and skills necessary to ensure both individual and community survival and wholeness. As the research has made amply clear, cooperative or collaborative learning does not mitigate individual initiative, worth, and achievement but rather provides a context where these necessary qualities are enhanced. But it is more. In a learning community not only do individuals learn survival and wholeness, but the community learns survival and wholeness as well.

The Ecology of Learning Communities

Learning communities don't just happen. Although the insight, knowledge, and skills for cooperative behavior are intuitive, because of our cultural programming to the contrary, learning communities must be carefully designed and deliberately nurtured. The ecological community is a natural and readily accessible model for a learning community. A pond community, a forest community, a prairie community — indeed, all communities in nature — are, at a fundamental level, learning communities in which individuals, species, and the community as a whole, learn, change, and grow. These communities share a set of essential properties characterized by the ecological principles identified in Chapter Six: interdependence, diversity, partnership, and co-evolution. Since I discussed these at some length earlier, here I will generalize on them by reflecting on the ecological features of a learning community as they apply to a classroom, a school, or a neighborhood.

1. *In a learning community, the curriculum is "Life in all of its manifestations."* The essence of education is learning about life through participation and relationship in community including not only people, but plants, animals, and the whole of nature. Thus, the primary resources are the lives, the experiences, relationships, questions, and concerns of the learners themselves.

2. *A learning community provides supportive, sensitive, valuing, responsive, accepting learning environments that enhance self-worth, creative intellectual endeavor, and responsible behavior.* Here one's contribution depends on what one brings to the experience and no one's personal worth is at stake. *Ownership, responsibility, and accountability are assumed to be synonymous with membership in the community.*

3. *A learning community is designed to reflect the interests and capabilities of the learner/students.* Because it is relevant to the interest and abilities of its members, the individual has as much power over her learning environment as she is capable of handling. Students are encouraged to learn on their own initiative and in as many diverse ways as possible.

4. *A learning community is cooperative and synergistic.* Here everyone is both a learner and a resource for everyone else. The outcomes are designed to challenge the intuition, imagination, knowledge, and skills of the members, including the instructor. Peer learning is heightened, and everyone recognizes that in many situations, two or more heads are truly better than one.

5. *A learning community extends beyond the walls of the classroom.* Because the curriculum reflects all the life experiences of the student, the community of learners is expanded to include other peers, administrators, support staff, parents, and members of the broader community.

6. *In a learning community, learning is participative so that feelings and intellect are fully involved in every facet of the learning process.* Learning is always experiential and relevant in ways that ensure the learner of participation in the decisions that shape her or his learning. In this way, both intuitive and cognitive processes and knowledge are honored, and learning experiences are designed to reflect the multidimensional and multisensory nature of intelligence, thinking, and learning.

7. *A learning community is characterized by both consistency and responsiveness.* Because the environment can be depended on, there is little or no anxiety and fear. When the learning environment is reactive, malleable, and responsive, students can actively participate in creating and shaping their learning experience.

8. *A learning community provides regular, consistent, and appropriate assessment through a variety of feedback loops.* The primary purpose of assessment is to provide qualitative feedback vis-à-vis progress toward clearly defined learning objectives in ways that tap the wellsprings of creative possibility inherent in each member of the community. Such assessment is nonjudgmental and noncompetitive.

9. *A learning community is energized by a shared purpose, vision, or*

mission. A purpose held in common can turn a random assortment of individual students who happen to be assigned to the same classroom into a genuine learning community. Shared visions are seldom imposed from above, e.g., by a teacher, but must emerge from the goals, aspirations, and dreams of the members themselves. A shared sense of purpose can create an alignment of energy that is empowering and energizing for everyone. In such cases, individual performance is often enhanced beyond predictable expectations.

Carole Cooper and Julie Boyd (1994), co-directors of Global Learning Communities, note that a collaborative learning community is

> a philosophy as well as a place; it is a way of being as well as a working model. It is a mindset as well as a map.... The foundation ... is *collaboration* — working together for common goals, partnership, shared leadership, co-evolving and co-learning — rather than competition and power given to only a few.

They remind us that "the focus of the collaborative learning community is *learning* ... [which] takes place within the context of *community.*" This is in contrast to the traditional classroom where the focus is on teaching, e.g., covering the content, and where students sit in quiet isolation presumably absorbing what is presented and taking written tests to prove it. In a classroom that has become a collaborative learning community, (1) students take responsibility for their own learning; (2) learning experiences are geared to students' interests and needs; (3) students are actively engaged in learning in a variety of groups and contexts; and (4) learning is understood, applied, demonstrated, and internalized (Cooper and Boyd, 1994). These characteristics are, of course, the very ones that I have been promoting throughout this book. They are ecological in nature and humanistic in principle. To embrace them requires a different set of assumptions about human nature and the fundamental relationships that shape our lives. To put it simply, they are the essence of a new and comprehensive paradigm.

Learning communities don't just happen. They reflect core values that are essentially the values of the community. The Center for the Study of Community in Santa Fe suggests some basic values that characterize creative, healthy learning communities (Cooper and Boyd 1994):

> Sense of shared values; agreement on core values; participation; communication; commitment; conscious choice; shared responsibility; eq-

uity; openness; respect for differences; acceptance; trust; collaboration; reciprocity; accountability; efficacy; perceived skill; and cohesion.

Imagine the difference it would make if every school in America were designed to reflect these values? The great irony is that we already have a model for learning communities that reflect all of these characteristics — the modern preschool or kindergarten. Visit a nearby kindergarten and note the ambiance: bright colors, lots of light from large windows, plenty of space, small unobtrusive learning centers designed for one or two students, small tables, bookcases and books, a warm carpet, and lots of pillows. There are also lots of toys: puzzles, pattern blocks, Cuisenaire rods, magnets, crayons, paints, paper, scissors. There may even be a couple of computers with fun games and creative tools for drawing, painting, and lettering. In some rooms you will find ladders for climbing and tunnels for crawling or hiding. There is a low murmur of conversation with other children and with the teacher who is unobtrusively moving around among the children. While a voice may occasionally be raised in excitement, in general the talk is "library talk" because the children are intensely involved in whatever they are doing. Look at their faces. They are alive and intent with concentration as they lie on the floor, lean across the table, or sit quietly in the corner with a book. In short, they are engrossed in whatever they are doing. Are they learning? Of course! Are they enjoying the experience? Of course. Are they a learning community? Of course.

After you've spent an hour in the kindergarten room, move on to the fourth or fifth grade classroom and spend an equal amount of time quietly sitting in the corner. Chances are that the children are sitting in rows either listening to the teacher or doing seat work. Either way, there is no talking. If there is a question, it's for clarification: "Do we have to write in complete sentences?" "Does punctuation count?" Any other verbal exchange is in answer to a teacher's question. In these cases, note which students answer the teacher's questions. Watch their faces. Then look at the faces of the other students. Note the difference between the faces of these children and those in kindergarten. In general, these faces are blank, the kids are passive and, except for an occasional wiggle or squirm, the kids are perfectly still. Count the number of kids who are daydreaming. How many are just plain bored? The teacher sits at a desk or walks up and down the aisle looking over the shoulders at the seat work, occasionally pointing out a mistake, a messy paper, or a misspelled word. Does the teacher look happy? How often does she smile? How often does she frown? If you want to know what's wrong with education today, figure out why there is such a difference between what's happening in kindergarten and what's happening — or not happening — in the fourth, or eighth, or tenth grade classroom. It's as simple — and as complex — as that!

By now it should be obvious that a "learning community" is not the same as a "community of learners." While educators may use the term "community" as a euphemism to describe the arbitrary assortment of individuals in a typical classroom or school, proximity doesn't automatically create community. And while the inclusion of cooperative learning activities may turn a classroom of individuals into a community of individual learners, it does not necessarily mean that they have become a learning community. As long as the emphasis in the classroom is *on the individual at the expense of community*, it can never be more than a collection of individual learners who may share some community-like experiences. In short, in a learning community, not only do the individuals who make up the community learn, change, and grow, but the community as a whole also learns, changes, and grows. As a result of the cooperative synergism of its members, the learning community thrives and moves in new directions with capacities that would be impossible without the common goals and shared leadership of its members. As the community changes and grows, the members of the community benefit in innumerable and often exciting ways.

The Classroom as a Learning Community

It is obvious that the ambience of a classroom as learning community is radically different from that of a traditional, individual-based classroom. For the past several years, teachers at Thompson Middle School have been encouraged to organize and conduct their classrooms and teams as collaborative learning communities. It is obvious to even the casual observer that the ambiance of these classrooms is radically different from that of a traditional, individual-based classroom. Special Education teacher Jan Sutfin reflects on the difference:

> I, along with my special students, have experienced something very unique and enlightening. We have experienced inclusion into an inte-

grated curriculum environment. It is an environment designed for learning at its deepest, most connected level. It is a place where learning opportunities abound and positive attitudes can't help but flourish. Sound like an unattainable ideal? Yes it does. But walk into a classroom where students are enthusiastically leaning in toward the center of their cooperative group sharing ideas, coming to consensus, and developing a plan; where there is an understanding that they are connected in powerful, wonder-filled ways by their unique talents, and you become a believer. Students with short attention spans get pulled into the action. Students who have difficulty expressing themselves begin to do so. Students who have difficulty writing have the confidence to record information for their group. A miracle is not occurring! However, something awesome is. People who have carried labels all their school lives suddenly don't have them any more. They too have something special to offer in this academic learning community. What they learn and how they learn it has relevance to them. Connections have been made that cause students to say, "I get it."

How does this environment develop? In this case, the "how" is attributed not to the teacher alone, but to the entire classroom community. After all, we are all connected; one cannot do it without the other.

This illustration reflects many of the ecological characteristics that characterize learning communities. Note, for example, how *interdependence* is expressed. It is obvious that the students understand implicitly that *the success of each individual member depends on the success of the team/community as a whole, while at the same time the success of the team/community depends on the success of each member*. They know that it is in everyone's best interest to see that everyone else succeeds. This is possible because in these teams everyone learns from everyone else. Rather than achieving a level of learning based on the lowest common denominator as often happens in other classrooms, the synergy of the team often quickens the insight, knowledge, and skills of even the brightest student and raises the level of learning to new heights for everyone. For example, special education teacher Jean Humke found that, given an appropriate environment, so-called youth-at-risk can survive.

I have seen the LD/BD students thrive in the integrated, cooperatively taught classroom. William was a bright boy with good auditory and mechanical reasoning skills, who could not read a traditional science textbook. In lab and group project work he became the leader. Someone else did the reading and the recording, and William took over the hands-on part. His motivation improved and negative classroom behaviors disappeared.

After the experience of having Jean's students integrated into her eighth grade science class, Bonnie Pettebone wrote,

> The surprise was seeing that the regular children also benefited from having the "specials" in the classroom. Although Jean kept an eye on her special students, she worked with the entire class. This was especially helpful for the lower ability students who didn't qualify for special education services. When special ed students were part of a group project, other "regular" students often came to the study hall where Jean gave her special ed students extra help. The room that was once the "LD room" — an embarrassment to the students assigned there — became just another classroom. Soon, regular students were asking if they could come all the time.

A second essential in a learning community is *diversity*. Although tracking students by ability level or long-term goal, e.g., gifted, or college bound, has a long history in schools, research makes it clear that diversity both in age and ability results in more stimulating and productive learning environments than are possible with homogeneous groupings. While cooperative learning provides a unique opportunity for mixed ability groups, many teachers who have had only a cursory introduction to cooperative learning still operate on the assumption that if good and poor students are in the same teams, the former will do all the work while the latter share in the success. At Thompson, however, it has been demonstrated over and again that this is not the case. When teams of students are free to explore their own questions in ways that they determine, each member learns to share in both the responsibilities and the benefits of team learning. Ownership of one's own learning is, after all, the most successful motivation possible. In addition, students are the best teachers and soon those who initially tend to be lazy learn to participate more fully. As noted in the last chapter, one sixth grade team at Thompson reports that since students began to define their focus of study, only 3 of 125 students were chronically choosing to do poor work — far fewer than in previous years.

In his year-end summary report to the teachers based on the meetings he had had with the various teams, Kurt Anderson reflects on some of things they, as a community, have learned.

> We are beginning to learn that there is no "right way." That's the exciting and frustrating part about it! Our commitment is to create and discover experiences that will be best for kids. As long as we have that goal and leverage what we learn from each other, we will reach the vision of "integrative learning" — whatever that is. I think we know it when we see it, but we can't get it into words just yet!!!!!!

As has already been noted, as a result of Thompson's inclusion program, special education students are now full participants in regular science and social studies classes at all levels. And they are not merely tolerated by other students. Last year an eighth grade "Learning Disabled" girl received the quarterly "team choice" award by her academic team based on her level of team participation. This was the first time an LD student had been selected for this award. In her end-of-the-year "A Celebration of Learning" report, seventh grade team leader Joanna Martin wrote, "The team has openly accepted special ed teacher and kids — something which couldn't have happened four years ago. The growth has been phenomenal. To watch a special ed child who we didn't think had any growth last year actively involved in dissecting a shark and anxious to get to a frog, has been most gratifying." Team leader Bonnie Pettebone noted that one of her special ed boys "walked in as a six-footer with four feet of confidence. Now he is confident and leading — why — because the process is the emphasis, not the final test." In the words of another teacher, "Instead of being considered outsiders, special ed students are often defended by regular students in the same way they defend their closest friends."

Another characteristic of learning communities experienced at Thompson is the countless forms of *partnership* strategies. These strategies reflect both cooperation and competition and involve students, teachers, teams, and the school as a whole. As a result of the new focus on cooperation, these groups *coevolve* through an interplay of creativity and mutual adaptation. For example, teams have been challenged by the opportunity to present their final product, e.g., a Medieval Fair, to the entire student body. On the other hand, the healthy but often subtle competition has stimulated some genuine risk-taking on the part of more reluctant student teams and teacher teams — a kind of "If they can do it, so can I" response.

The learning communities at Thompson are energized by the *free flow of information,* and the built-in *feedback loops* have been increasingly effective because of the cooperative groupings. Almost without exception, teachers consider the primary purpose of assessment to be feedback to students and have created a variety of assessment rubrics designed to accomplish this. Although teachers are still required to give grades, instead of being stuck with a final grade, students are encouraged to redo for improvement — a process that truly enhances the learning. Teachers who still give quizzes and tests find that having students "take quizzes until you get it right — along with reminder hints during the quizzes — has really promoted the learning." In some classes, anything below a B is a "do-over." For one team, math assessment is now displayed through portfolios, not homework and tests." Finally, "they are not the same kids at the end of the year. Because of 'do and redo,' grades are higher and more kids have learned more things better." This year teams will be given the option of including with the grade narrative reports from teachers. Donna's seventh grade team has decided that each grade they give will be accompanied by a brief account of the student's experience and progress in that subject.

Feedback works both ways. One seventh grade teacher noted, "The kids have directed things a lot. When they see that we have listened to them and used the feedback they gave us — when they notice you have changed based on what they have said, they have great ideas and suggestions."

Sustainability in learning communities requires both different and a greater variety of resources than those usually found in the traditional school. Most schools are still more like "ecological monocultures," e.g., a cornfield, than ecological communities, e.g., a prairie. Just as prairies or forests require a greater variety of resources than a cornfield, so it is with schools that are becoming learning communities. As Resource Center Director Chris Sherman notes, this is occurring at Thompson.

> Kids ... are exploring subjects for which relatively few materials have been available. *The result is that different kinds of resources are being ordered to meet the needs of both teachers and students.*(emphasis added).

I think the following insight, shared by Eva Pierrakos, co-founder of the Pathways Community in upstate New York, captures the essence of the ecology of learning communities.

> The group consciousness does not level off uniqueness, but furthers it. The group is no longer used as a crutch because the self cannot handle life. Nor is the group an authority that one needs to rebel against.... The highest organization of group consciousness is that within which each individual has found ... autonomy. (Davidson and Davidson 1994)

Such a classroom is not an accidental happenstance, the result, say, of one of those truly outstanding classes that appear on rare occasions. Although the cooperative characteristics are intuitive, the classroom environment must be thoughtfully and carefully designed. Teachers must not only understand, but must experience for themselves what it means to belong to a learning community. Recognizing this need for an experiential introduction to cooperative learning, for the past three years the St. Charles schools have provided a series of week-long workshops and in-class training sessions in cooperative learning with Carole Cooper. Although attendance at these has been voluntary, most teachers have attended at least one such workshop. Many have participated in two or more and several teachers have become skilled trainers in their own right so that the district can now offer its own in-service training programs. As a result, the entire faculty of Thompson has become experientially grounded in both the philosophy and methodologies of cooperative, or what Carole Cooper prefers to call collaborative, learning.

When I first went to Thompson, I found it taken for granted that for most studies, students would be divided through a variety of combinations into learning groups or teams of four. These teams were characterized by the four elements common to cooperative learning classes — positive interdependence, face-to-face interaction among students, individual accountability for mastery, and interpersonal and small group skills (Johnson et al. 1984). The following report by eighth grade teacher Barb Gudvangen, reflects the general ambience of Thompson. Due to illness, Barb was two months late in starting school. She records her experience.

> I was amazed at how well the cooperative groups were functioning. At first I thought I would have to work at gaining control of the classes. But I found control to be no problem at all. I attributed this to three factors. One was the excellent work the other team members had already done with these students. A second factor was heterogeneous grouping. The third factor was the work done earlier by the sixth and seventh grade teachers who had been trained in cooperative learning.

During my first curriculum workshop, it was clear from the ease with which the teachers worked together that there was a level of cooperation among workshop participants that I had not found in other schools. In the succeeding months, I realized that the training in cooperative learning had prepared the rich and fertile soil within which creative and innovative strategies, such as the integrated curriculum, process writing, whole language, authentic evaluation, and outcome-oriented learning, have found root and are flourishing. Without the plowing and tilling generated by the philosophy and experiential methodologies of cooperative learning, the hard ground, though extremely fertile, is often so inhospitable that only the occasional seed can grow.

Principal Kurt Anderson was reminded of the importance of such preparation when he recently visited another district to introduce them to what was taking place at Thompson. On several occasions, he asked his audience of teachers and administrators to form teams for the purpose of discussion. He was amazed at the level of resistance and their reluctance to work together or to discuss anything of substance. In contrast, on almost any occasion if one walks into the teachers' lounge at Thompson, one can hear substantive conversations about what's happening in the classrooms — even including the failures. It is not unusual to hear excited voices describing classroom experiences that would have been unthinkable a few years earlier.

As a consequence of this training in cooperative learning, while there is still resistance to substantive changes on the part of some teachers, many of the interdisciplinary, grade-level teams at Thompson have become genuine collaborative learning communities. Even those teams that have resisted changes in the orientation of the curriculum are, to a significant extent, applying cooperative learning strategies in their classrooms. From the perspective of an outside observer, it is clear that the levels of energy, enthusiasm, synergy, creativity, and, not so incidently, laughter are very high. One has only to walk through the halls and look into the classrooms to know that Thompson is different from most other schools.

Ruth Ann Dunton describes her team's experience:

I realized that it was through "systems" and the functions therein that the fundamental concepts are inherent. If students understand what a system is and how it works, they are able to understand and apply concepts such as diversity, interdependence, sustainability, change, etc., naturally. So, we introduced students to systems and have been using [the systems] matrix in many ways. Together, we — teachers and students, teachers and teachers, students and students — are doing some serious thinking. All of us on the team have been experimenting with the systems models in different ways. We feel that we have reached a new level of thinking, but that we are truly just beginning to explore the possibilities. We are impressed with the ideas the children have. At the same time we realize that we need to continue to work together as a team — always pushing ourselves to a higher level. Only in this way can we better facilitate in our classrooms. We are not always sure of ourselves. Sometimes we become exhausted from thinking, but it's that good kind of exhausted when you're exhilarated at the same time. We feed on each other's ideas and need more time to explore our thoughts. We feel we are the students in a student-centered situation. Truly, we as a team find ourselves in a "learning community" situation which is what I have been hoping for all along. Hurrah!

The School as a Learning Community

As we have discovered at Thompson, when classrooms become genuine learning communities, the school itself is in the process of becoming a learning community. One model for the school as a learning community is the learning organization. Based on the work of Peter Senge (1990) and other corporate consultants, the learning organization provides an effective and practical prototype for organizational transformation from within. According to Senge, the learning organization is one

> where people continually expand their capacity to create the results they truly desire, where new and expansive patterns of thinking are nurtured, where collective aspiration is set free, and where people are continually learning how to learn together.... The organization that will truly excel in the future will be the organization that discovers how to tap people's commitment and capacity to learn at *all* levels in an organization.

One of the characteristics of the learning organization is that the *customer* is recognized as integral to the organization. For example, there are many parallels between the failure of Ford and General Motors and Honda's success in the 1970s and the failure of public schools during the last 20 years. In much the same way that Ford and GM believed they knew best what people wanted/needed — namely what Ford and GM wanted to produce, e.g., big cars — so educators believe that they know best what students want/need — namely what educators want to teach. On the other hand, Honda was a genuine learning organization that listened to their customers and responded by designing the kinds of cars they wanted. When a school becomes a learning community, its entire focus is designed to respond to the learners' needs. In short, the entire school is truly learner-centered. This focus on the customer has been one of the lessons that teachers and administrators at St. Charles learned from a series of Total

Quality Management (TQM) seminars conducted by Arthur Andersen & Co. Kurt Anderson comments on this influence.

> Our training in Total Quality Management helped us recognize the need for our work to be "customer-driven," "consumer-focused." For our immediate concerns, the students and their parents are our customers. Education is unique in that the primary customer is also the primary worker in the system. Suffice it to say that the student should come first in all our thinking. Now this philosophy permeates all our thinking — from scheduling, to delivery of instruction, from extracurricular opportunities to bussing.
>
> On the other hand, we are also recognizing that teachers are also customers — that is, we are all learners.

Kurt is quick to point out that Thompson's mission statement is the only one he has ever seen that mentions adults. It begins with the words, "Thompson Middle School is committed to nurturing and involving students and adults.... " Reflecting on this inclusion, Kurt commented:

> The first and foremost goal of staff development is to help teachers become healthy individuals. If we are healthy people inside this building, we will have healthy kids. If we aren't healthy ourselves, it doesn't matter what kind of curriculum or teaching strategies we have because only healthy individuals can allow and help kids make healthy choices.

It must be emphasized once again, however, that the fundamental issue here is not content versus no content, nor is it adults' content versus students' content. The issue revolves around the real-life needs of the consumers of educational expertise.

However, schools are unique organizations in that their students are not the only customers whose needs must be addressed. Parents are also customers and, indirectly, so is the larger community that the school serves. Thus, when we talk about the school as a learning community, we must include parents and others of the larger community among its members. In short, even as the one-room school of yesteryear often served as the hub of community activities, so this function is, I believe, implicit in the concept of schools in a democratic society. If schools are to become learning communities in which *all of its members* are, to some degree, learners, then the walls of the school must become permeable and true centers of learning for the entire community. This can be accomplished in a variety of ways, such as evening classes and other activities that address adult needs.

One elementary school with which I worked several years ago provides an outstanding illustration of how the school can become a vehicle for creating community both within and beyond its four walls. Asa Messer Elementary School in Providence, Rhode Island, was a pilot school for Ecoliteracy, an ecologically based educational program that Fritjof Capra, Carole Cooper, and I designed as a model for restructuring education. Substantively, Ecoliteracy is modeled on and incorporates the philosophy and strategies presented in this book. During the course of a year, Carole Cooper and I conducted a series of workshops for the Asa Messer teachers. An inner-city neighborhood school, Asa Messer draws its students from a widely diverse ethnic and cultural milieu — more than 40 languages are spoken by the 92% minority families of its students. All school–family communications are printed in three languages, English, Cambodian, and Spanish.

The Providence Public Schools, like any large urban school district, suffers from the complex problems inherent in any bureaucracy. Giving lip service to school-based change is far easier than supporting it. Our Ecoliteracy team soon realized that the staff at Asa Messer were highly skeptical of and resistant to any new ideas — particularly when these ideas were introduced by what they interpreted to be administrative flat. The protection of turf was endemic and resistance to any form of change was palpable. They had been burned so often and were wary of anything different. There were times when we became convinced that the only thing the teachers agreed on was a shared lack of trust in anything new or different. And yet, beneath their skepticism, we found that the teachers were deeply concerned, they did care for their children, often going out of their way to work with those who were having problems. In the words of Principal Jerry Landies, "We have to be mothers, fathers, sisters, brothers, policemen, doctors, lawyers — and fit that all into the school day, as well as curriculum. So for some teachers, [Ecoliteracy] was just another thing they were being asked to do" (Cleland 1994). Dedicated to his work and desperately overloaded with the administrative trivia common to large bureaucracies, Jerry gave us complete cooperation and support within the limits of bureaucratic constraints.

During the summer preceding our involvement with Asa Messer, I had become acquainted with a unique program being conducted in rural

Vermont called Food Works. Helping students and parents work cooperatively to design and build vegetable gardens that became "curriculum
organizers," this program assisted schools in designing integrated curricu-
lums based on ecological and cultural concepts that were indigenous to the
area. As we began to realize that the Asa Messer teachers needed some kind
of practical, hands-on program that enabled them and their students to
actually experience the ecological principles we had introduced, I recommended that the teachers consider some kind of garden project similar to
Food Works. Shortly thereafter, due to lack of funding and bureaucratic turf
battles, Carole and I discontinued our personal association with the program. However, the idea gained support and, using local resources, the
garden project began to evolve. The following report was written a year
later by principal Jerry Landies.

> To get the ball rolling, students and teachers built garden boxes with
> the help of community members. Teachers then began to formulate
> math lessons based on the planting of seeds and drew from farming
> folk tales and garden fables for their reading lessons. Weaving the
> educational requirements into the larger framework of Ecoliteracy
> began to make sense.... The more the teachers began to do these
> projects, the more they realized ... you don't do Ecoliteracy on Monday
> morning from 9:00 to 11:00 and do math from 11:00 to 12:00 and do
> English the rest of the day. You can combine it all; it's all one philosophy.

> With the help of parents, volunteers, teachers, school administrators
> and local politicians, Asa Messer's 625 students enthusiastically under-
> took a hugely successful neighborhood cleanup near the end of the
> school year. The effort drew support from community members and
> businesses and brought the school neighborhood together. These was
> especially significant because the majority of Asa Messer students are
> from Cambodia, where reverent parents normally stay away from
> involvement with their children's school.... Many of the Cambodians
> maintain small garden plots in their own crowded Providence neigh-
> borhoods and bring several millennia of native wisdom about the land
> — resources that will add immeasurably to the school's gardening and
> cultural awareness efforts.

Landies concluded,

> We developed some good will through the clean-up day.... Just the
> feedback alone was tremendous. It gave the kids themselves a sense of
> *being*, that they had actually made a contribution that people appreci-
> ated.... We started out by learning the principles of ecology, but hearing
> them and really believing them are not necessarily the same thing....
> [Ecoliteracy] is something that you have to experience.

National Education Association President Keith Geiger (1995) has recognized this important function of the school in the community.

> The breakdown of community underlies much of what afflicts America today — drugs and despair, complacency and indifference, discrimination and bigotry, violence and rancor. We cannot return to the one-room schoolhouses that communities literally build with their bare hands. But we can begin to reinvigorate our communities by making our public schools truly community schools — ones in which everyone has ownership.... In the community public schools, citizens, parents, teachers, support personnel, principals, and businesspeople pull together to make a uniquely American institution work.... We return to the idea of the community public school not because it is old, but because it is true. When schools are the center of the community, as Thomas Jefferson envisioned, we have better schools and better communities.

"Make A Difference Day" was a step in the direction of involving the Thompson school community more directly in the larger community. Although individual classes had, from time to time, taken on community-oriented projects, this was the first time the entire school had participated. Since the day was an early release day with classes ending at noon, it was decided that teachers and students would spend the entire morning implementing the projects that their teams had chosen. Team projects included making sack lunches for a local homeless shelter, packed in individually decorated brown bags; conducting a river cleanup on the Fox River, which runs through the middle of St. Charles; helping with a local prairie restoration project, e.g., collecting seeds; undertaking school grounds clean-up; having a clothing drive; making and presenting paper-flower corsages with individual notes to residents of a local nursing home; conducting a community-based food drive for the township Food Pantry; and making and distributing handcrafts and individualized letters to members of a local retirement center. The enthusiasm and excitment permeated the entire building. A district administrator who happened to be visiting the school that day described the ambience as magical.

Designing Schools as Learning Communities

Economist David Korten (1995) echos the central theme of this chapter when he notes,

> Healthy societies depend on healthy, empowered local communities that build caring relationships among people and help us connect to a par-

ticular piece of the living Earth with which our lives are intertwined. Such societies must be built through local-level action, household by household and community by community.

Korten might have added, "school by school." I believe that schools are the most obvious places to begin re-creating community — first in the classrooms, and simultaneously within the school itself among the teachers, staff, and students. But, as happened at Asa Messer, the community that is centered in the school can be expanded to incorporate the broader neighborhood of parents, neighbors, friends, and businesspeople. Only in this way can parents once again reclaim their right to educate their children in schools that reflect and honor their values, beliefs, and standards.

For this to happen, schools must once again become community-based and neighborhood-oriented. This means that in the future, schools must be smaller rather than larger and may well be racially, ethnically, and culturally homogeneous. While this seemingly contradicts the ecological principle of diversity as well as the goals of cultural diversity espoused by many Americans, I suggest that it may actually be more ecological than our present legal interpretation of diversity and more educationally beneficial than many of our marginally integrated schools. It is significant, I think, that at the very time when schools and communities need neighborhood schools as a community focal point, the Supreme Court has eased the federal regulations that forced large metropolitan school districts to desegregate their schools by bussing. While I initially supported bussing as a necessary way to integrate and equalize educational opportunity, I think the time has now come when the need to re-create sustainable neighborhoods and communities is greater than the need to integrate every school. When separation is by choice and financial resources are distributed equitably, everyone — children, families, schools, neighborhoods, and communities — will benefit from neighborhood schools.

This means that large public school districts must eventually decentralize into several smaller districts, while these districts must decentralize to the extent that substantive control and direction is provided by the community which is served by the school. In this way, neighborhood schools need not stand alone but can be linked within districts whose primary function is to provide a variety of support services but without the large bureaucratic systems that traditionally have accompanied such services. This is possible if the districts are designed from the bottom up so that the primary decisions, including allocation of monies, will always be made in the school by those whose lives are affected by the decisions. As NEA President Keith Geiger (1995) notes,

> The community public school is the opposite of the factory-style, remote controlled school.... In the community public school, citizens, parents, teachers, support personnel, principals, and businesspeople pull together to make a uniquely American institution work.

In this way, the function of school districts changes radically. No longer in control, districts can serve as resources, encouraging networking among schools and providing services at the request of the community schools. This will, of course, require that principals once again become educational leaders rather than building managers, a role that, unfortunately, many prefer. It will also require that local citizens learn the self-governing skills necessary for participative, nonauthoritarian leadership. For those who say this is an impossible task, I would remind them that, as Paul Hawken suggests, it is simply a matter of design.

In fact, this model is already being implemented. Geiger cites the example in Seattle, where administrators, parents, and citizens worked cooperatively to trim the system's central bureaucracy by 40%. By eliminating all layers of management between the superintendent and the principals, they saved millions of dollars that they promptly reinvested in the schools.

There are several advantages to the small neighborhood school, most of which are obvious. The neighborhood provides a "sense of place" — a concept that is fundamental to indigenous educational practice but which is almost totally foreign to current American education where the same textbook content is being studied in a dozen different states and thousands of different schools. A sense of place includes an already established community and the opportunity for active parental involvement and local control. It includes, where appropriate, the school being available as a year-round community/social/learning center for learners of all ages. Another advantage that seems to be increasingly important is that neighborhood schools can become centers of cultural, ethnic, or racial identity and pride. Though a given neighborhood may lack a broad diversity of social groups that for some may seem to be important, there is a wonderful opportunity for schools to proudly reflect the mores, values, and standards of the local community as they did a century ago. If the parents in one neighborhood prefer to have sex education while the parents in another prefer not to, each can be governed according to parental desires. A school can include locally important ethnic or racial programs, e.g., Black Studies, Cambodian Studies, etc., without every school in the district having to adopt the same curriculum. There is still diversity but it is now at a different level — a diversity of schools within a single district. When a district is structured in this way, students can, through a voucher system, be given the freedom to switch to another school within the same district.

Along with this freedom of choice comes a new level of accountability — schools that are constantly losing students to other schools are obviously not meeting the needs of their constituencies and will, of necessity, be forced to change or close.

There are two perceived disadvantages to such homogeneity and both are related to finances. The first is that the local community may not have an adequate tax base. Once again, it depends upon how the system is designed. An areawide, citywide, or statewide program designed to level the financial support for schools would solve this problem and insure that separate can be equal, if the separation is by choice and not by manipulation or law. The more serious perceived disadvantage is that large buildings can have better facilities than smaller ones — facilities such as gyms, lunchrooms, resource centers, and science and computer labs. I would argue that while such amenities are nice, they are neither necessary nor important enough to offset the advantages of small, neighborhood-based schools — particularly at the elementary level. However, I'm not convinced this is an either/or issue. Once schools become community centers where everyone in the community can participate in a variety of continuing education programs, schools will be open all the time, and will, therefore, be more likely to engender the financial support necessary to meet the needs not only of children but of the entire community.

Another feature of the traditional, one-room school-as-community that is slowly regaining acceptance is the multi-level classroom. We now know that kids learn a great deal from their peers and that students-teaching-students is one of the best ways to learn — for both the one teaching and the one being taught. It is ridiculous to assume that because a student is 12 years old, she or he automatically is ready for sixth grade-level work in all the subject areas. For those who believe in the *school as factory* model — where everything, including classrooms, must be organized into neat, discrete categories that follow some preset criteria — proposals such as multilevel classes will be considered a throwback to preindustrial times. However, for those who understand human developmental processes and who appreciate the informal ways that people learn and that communities function, multi-level classrooms will seem like an idea whose time has come — or, more accurately, has come again.

Another feature of the *school-as-community* that Kurt Anderson is implementing involves students in the care and upkeep of the school building and grounds. As a result of an experience last year when two students who were conducting an ecological audit of the school's utilization of natural resources recommended changes that were, in the long run, highly cost effective, Kurt requested and recently received administrative approval to have students perform much of the routine custodial work previously performed by two custodians. The money that was saved went into curricular resources requested by the teachers and resource center director. There is nothing better than participation in care to create a sense of ownership and a sense of place for students who spend so much of their day in school.

The High School as a Learning Community

While most parents today expect preschool to be a fun experience for children and some may even agree that elementary and middle schools should be enjoyable, satisfying experiences, influenced as they are by their own educational experience, few would be comfortable if classrooms for 16-year-olds resembled kindergarten. Communities are willing to build elaborate labs and expensive recreational facilities for their high schools, but when it comes to classrooms, the only acceptable design is the factory model with its inflexible structure, its production-line mentality, and the inevitable memorize-and-recall mode of learning. If, however, we accept the assumption that the best curriculum at any level is student-centered, then we must begin to rethink the role and function of the American high school. As Roberts and Cawelti (1984) note, there is no clear consensus on what the central mission of the high school should be. "Critics have long lamented the fact that high schools have tried to do far more than they could reasonably expect to accomplish and as a result have diluted the academic program."

In earlier chapters I have suggested that to adequately prepare students for life in the twenty-first century, e.g., learning how to learn, the fundamental purpose and role of the education must be transformed. This transformation must include the high school as well as lower grades. However, until we recognize the discrepancies that exist between the knowledge and skills for learning how to learn and the so-called world class standards that currently dominate high school outcomes, nothing substantive will change. These discrepancies highlight the constraints that must be addressed before substantive change can take place at this level.

For example, much of today's high school curriculum is based on the outdated assumption that once children achieve the capacity for abstract thinking and reasoning — Piaget's "formal operations" — learning no longer needs to be concrete or relevant. Nothing could be further from the truth. Regardless of age, true learning must always be relevant to the life experience of the learner. The lack of concern for relevance is reflected in the factory-model mindset, which assumes that students can switch their cognitive gears every 45 minutes — shifting from math to social studies to science to literature to physical education — all before lunch.

But relevance is only one facet of learning. As I pointed out in Chapter Two, everything that we know about thinking and learning, intelligence and the structure of knowledge, points to one conclusion: *all intellectual endeavor, regardless of age, is systemic and contextual.* In short, facts are not the building blocks of knowledge, but its fruit. The process is not linear but organic. The outcome is not an end that has been or will be achieved, but a process to be experienced hour by hour, minute by minute. Learning is not something that can be taught; it is as natural as breathing, eating, running, or playing. Mary Catherine Bateson (1994) speaks of learning as "one of life's greatest pleasures." Once we acknowledge this, we will, in her words, "cease to focus on learning as preliminary and see it threaded through other layers of experience ... an open-ended introduction to a process of continual change in which self-observation can become the best of teachers."

A second constraint to substantive change at the high school level is the problem of scheduling. Exacerbated in large schools by the sheer size of the student body and the diverse multiplicity of offerings, the schedule has become the primary structural barrier to change. However, once the school's mission becomes clear, appropriate scheduling becomes essentially a design problem that can be remedied.

The last constraint may be more difficult to overcome: resistance on the part of teachers who have a significant investment both in their specialized disciplines and in the independence that accompanies such specialization. For this reason, Roberts and Cawelti recognize that substantive change will necessitate a substantial program of professional development that involves the teachers directly in redesigning the curriculum. However, on every high school faculty there are a few teachers who are ready and eager to attempt innovative programs. For example, at St. Charles High School several interested teachers have been given permission to design team-led, interdisciplinary courses. At a neighboring high school, located in a major river valley, a science and a social studies teacher have received permission to offer a course based on the question, "How have rivers shaped American culture?" Because of back-to-back scheduling, the course will be conducted daily for 90 minutes and will include significant blocks of time for on-site investigations.

I think it is clear that, in time, high schools must find ways to adapt the middle school model, i.e., a team of four or five teachers with 100 to 125 students, to their unique requirements. One inner-city high school with whom I have worked initiated just such a program for 120 incoming freshman. While there were many adjustments to make, the major problem the five teachers faced was resistance from their colleagues. At the same time, however, it is significant to note that adults outside the educational system are beginning to support such a change. In a recent survey of more than 2000 respondents, 62% agreed that large schools should be broken into smaller communities (Friendly Exchange 1995).

Conclusion

The 1960s were the halcyon days for education. Educational reform was in the air. Workshops in New Math, Kitchen Physics, and "Man: A Course of Study" were popular among teachers at all levels, and schools were being designed and redesigned to accommodate the open classroom and experiential learning. Books like *Teaching as a Subversive Activity* and *Summerhill* were being discussed and debated among parents as well as teachers.

In 1968, George Leonard, a senior editor for *Look,* wrote a little book entitled *Education and Ecstasy.* As a professional journalist and therefore an outsider to education, Leonard's insightful combination of analysis and vision captured the essence of developmentally appropriate education. In the chapter, "Visiting Day, 2001 A.D.," Leonard sketches his vision of a school of the future. The school is a campus rather than a building. There are no formal classrooms and no teachers as we know them today. There are, however a variety of learning centers or, more accurately, learning environments, where children can read, play, listen, contemplate, sing, dance, create art, participate in individualized computer instruction — all according to the student's inclination. Early on, students are encouraged to respond to their own internal rhythms rather than clocks, schedules, and bells.

The underlying assumption of Leonard's vision is obvious. *Learning is as natural as breathing.* Learning is as much fun as exploring a cave — as exhilarating as a wild dance, as stimulating as a mystery thriller, as challenging as Nintendo, as satisfying as discovering a new friend with whom you can share your deepest thoughts and dearest secrets. Just as every child loves to explore caves, dance in the streets, mold clay, paint pictures, sing songs, tell and listen to stories, ask questions, imagine answers, they can also thrill in the discovery of the beauty and structure of math equations and chemical formulas, the intricacies of cell structure or of an atom or of a city, the possibilities and nuances of language and communication patterns, and the emotional impact of history (his-story) and her-story.

In spite of the obvious logic of Leonard's assumption, we continue to have a cultural predisposition against the idea that learning can be exciting, satisfying, and just plain enjoyable. For most people, learning is considered to be serious work, and, though it is not stated explicitly, the school is, more often than not, equated with the workplace. Since surveys show that most Americans do not like their jobs or their places of work, which are, to a great extent, dehumanizing environments, it should not be surprising that schools are also dehumanizing environments. And that's the problem: We as a society have become so conditioned to living and working in dehumanizing environments — schools, factories, offices, stores, restaurants, crowded cities, and equally crowded suburbs, high-rises, and ghettos — that we can scarcely imagine alternatives. Whenever we are confronted with a vision of something different and more satisfying, we justify our present reality with a "Yes, but this is the real world!" And so, we continue to inflict that same dehumanizing environment on our children day after day for twelve years or more, and we wonder why so many of them either fail or rebel. The reality is that in general, both our schools and our workplaces are what Leslie Hart would call "brain antagonistic" environments.

The irony is, of course, that all of Leonard's assumptions about human potential, thinking, and learning have, since then, been supported and expanded by research in many different fields. Indeed, these assumptions are the cornerstone of the integrated, learner-centered strategies presented here. Unfortunately, as is often the case with visionaries, Leonard's projected time frame was far too optimistic. What is important, however, is not his time frame, but the vision itself, at the heart of which is the recognition that, at the most fundamental of levels, education is about students, not curriculum.

Buckminister Fuller once observed, "Nature is clearly intent on making humans successful" (Golding 1995). The degree to which we as a species have achieved success is debatable. While we have literally taken over and remade the planet in our own image, it seems increasingly clear that to be successful in the future will require something more of us than just scientific and technological prowess.

It should be clear by now that I consider educational success to involve a great deal more than preparing our youth for jobs in a highly technological society. It is about far more than American competitiveness in what seems to be a dog-eat-dog world. Today, in the last decade of the twentieth century, educational success is about what it means to be human in a world gone awry. It is about human potential — about our hopes, our aspirations, our dreams, our visions. Today educational success is about the future — our kids' future and the future of their kids and their grandkids to the seventh generation. It may even be about the future of humankind on Planet Earth.

The theoretical formulations necessary to redesign a systemic educational structure that reflects our innately human process of meaning-making are already available. According to systems thinking the same theories and principles that were applicable at the micro level, e.g., curriculum design and learning strategies, can be applied at the macro level of institutional purpose, function, and structure. If we combine Taba's taxonomy of knowledge, Howard Gardner's work on multiple intelligences, the research that demonstrates the contextual nature of thinking and learning, Piaget's insights on cognitive development, and what we know about learning communities, we have a blueprint for designing a "brain-compatible" educational system.

Anthropologist Mary Catherine Bateson (1994) sums up the challenge which we as educators — and as humans — face today.

> We are called to join in a dance whose steps must be learned along the way.... Improvisation and new learning are not private processes, they are shared with others at every age ... so it is important to attend and respond. Even in uncertainty, we are responsible for our own steps.

References

Barker, J., 1990. *The power of vision*. Charter House Learning Corporation (Video).

Bateson, M. C. 1994. *Peripheral visions: Learning along the way*. New York: HarperCollins.

Berman, M. 1984. *The reenchantment of the world*. New York: Bantam.

Bloom, B. 1984, May. The Search for Methods of Group Instruction as Effective as One-to-One Tutoring. *Educational Leadership*.

Botkin, J. et al. 1979. *No limits to learning: Bridging the human gap*. New York: Pergamon.

Bowers, C. 1993. *Education, cultural myths, and the ecological crisis*. Albany: SUNY Press.

Boyer E., and D. Levine. n.d. *A quest for common learning*. Washington, DC: Carnegie Foundation for the Advancement of Teaching.

Brady, M. 1989. *What's worth teaching?* Albany: SUNY Press.

Briggs, J., and F. D. Peat. 1989. *Turbulent mirror*. New York: Harper and Row.

Brooks, J. G., and M. G. Brooks. 1993. *The Case for Constructivist Classrooms*. Alexandria, VA: Association for Supervision and Curriculum Development.

Brown, L. 1994. Forward, in *State of the world 1994*. Washington, DC: Worldwatch Institute.

Bruner, J. 1960. *The process of education*, New York: Random House/Vintage.

Cajete, G. 1994. *Look to the mountains: An ecology of indigenous education*. Durango: CO: Kivaki.

Cambourne, B. 1989, August. Paper presented at the Whole Language Umbrella Conference, St. Louis.

Capra, F., E. Clark, and C. Cooper. 1993. *Guide to ecoliteracy*. Berkeley: Elmwood Institute.

Capra, F. 1994. Ecoliteracy. Paper presented at conference on Whole School Change Based on Ecological Principles, 24-26 January, in San Francisco.

Carlson E., and R. P. Hey. 1994, December. Mitchell fires off a parting message. *AARP Bulletin*.

Cleland, T. 1994, Spring. Ecoliteracy: Building Community in Schools. *Elmwood Quarterly*, (10)1.

Cooper, C., and J. Boyd. 1995. Schools As Collaborative Learning Communities. *Cooperative Learning Magazine*, 15(1).

Coomer, J. 1981. *Quest for a sustainable society*. New York: Pergamon.

Davidson, G., and C. McLaughlin. 1995, June 4. Integrating the Spiritual and Political. New Dimensions Radio, NPR.

Davis, S. 1979, January. The case of the missing management model. *Graduate Review.*

Drucker, P. 1989. *The new realities*. New York: Harper and Row.

Ellison, L. 1990, Fall. What Does the Brain Have to do With Learning? *Holistic Education Review* 3(3): 41–46.

Etzioni, A. 1993. *The spirit of community*, New York: Crown.

Fogarty, R. 1992. If Mind Truly Matters: The Integrated Curriculum. In *If mind matters*, Vol. 1, ed. Arthur Costa, James Bellanca, and Robin Fogarty. Paletine, IL: Skylight.

Friendly Exchange. 1995, Winter. "Readers Want To Get Touch" *Friendly Exchange.*

Gardner, H. 1984. *Frames of mind*. New York: Basic Books.

Geiger, K. 1995, October 9-15. Mr. Jefferson Would be Pleased. *The Washington Post National Weekly Edition.*

Gibbons, K. 1995, April 23. Quoted in a sermon on "The Teaching Church," at the DuPage Unitarian Universalist Church, Naperville, Illinois.

Goetz D., and J. Janz. 1987, June. (Statement of Curriculum Writing Team). What Does It Mean to Grow Up in a Global Village? Beaver Dam, WI: United Catholic Parish Schools.

Golding, B. 1995, Autumn. A Fuller Universe: Bucky's Memory. *New Dimensions.*

Gregorc, A. 1985. *Inside styles, beyond the basics*. Maynard, MA: Gabriel Systems.

Gurley, L. I. 1982. Use of Gowin's vee and concept mapping strategies to teach responsibility for learning in high school biological sciences. Ph.D. diss, Cornell University.

Hardin, G. 1972. *Exploring new ethics for survival*. New York: Penguin.

Harman, W. 1988. *Global mind change*, Indianapolis: Knowledge Systems.

Hart, L. 1983. *Human brain and human learning*. New York: Longman.

Hawken, P. 1993. *The ecology of commerce*. New York: HarperBusiness.

Heller, J. 1994. *Closing time*. New York: Simon & Schuster.

Highwater, J. 1981. *The primal mind*. New York: Meridian/Penguin.

Hirsh, Jr., E. D. 1987. *Cultural literacy*. Boston: Houghton-Mifflin.

Howard, N. 1980, January. Probing the Creative Spark. *Dun's Review.*

Jacobs, J. 1992. *Systems of survival: A dialogue on the moral foundations of commerce and politics*, New York: Vintage Books/Random House.

Jacobs, H. H, ed. 1989. *Interdisciplinary curriculum: Design and implementation*. Alexandria, VA: Association for Supervision and Curriculum Development.

Johnson, D. W. et al. 1984. *Circles of learning*. Alexandria, VA: Association for Supervision and Curriculum Development.

Kaplan R. 1994, February. The coming anarchy. *Atlantic Monthly*.

Keen, S. 1991. *Fire In the belly*. New York: Bantam.

Keen, S. 1994. *Hymns to an unknown god*. New York: Bantam.

Kersey, K. 1983. *Sensitive parenting*. Washington, DC: Acropolis.

Kohn, A. 1986. *No context*. Boston: Houghton-Mifflin.

Korten, D. 1995. *When corporations rule the world*. West Hartford, CT: Kumanrian and San Francisco: Berrett-Koehler.

Lasch, C. 1995. *The revolt of the elites and the betrayal of democracy*. New York: Norton.

Leonard, G. 1968. *Education and Ecstacy*. New York: Delta/Dell.

Loye, D. 1983. *The sphinx and the rainbow*. Boulder: Shambhala.

Maver, D. 1991. Presentation at GATE training program, Minneapolis.

McLaughlin, C., and G. Davidson. 1994. *Spiritual politics: Changing the world from inside out*. New York: Ballantine.

Naisbitt, J. 1982. *Megatrends*. New York: Warner.

Nasbitt, J., and P. Aburdene. 1990. *Megatrends 2000*. New York: Morrow.

National Commission on Excellence in Education. 1983. *A nation at risk*. Washington: U. S. Department of Education.

Novak, J.D., and D.B. Gowin. 1984. *Learning how to learn*. Cambridge: Cambridge University Press.

Orr, D. 1993. The problem of discipline/The discipline of problems. *Holistic Education Review* 6(3).

Osborne, H. 1970. *Aesthetics and arts theory: An historical introduction*. New York: Dutton.

Pearce, J. C. 1980. *The magical child*. New York: Bantam.

Peck, M. S. 1987. *The different drum: Community making and peace*. New York: Simon & Schuster.

Perkins, D., and G. Salomon. 1992. The science and art of transfer. In *If minds matter*. Palatine, IL: Skylight Publishing.

Purpel, D. 1989. *The moral and spiritual crisis in education*. New York: Bergin and Garvey.

Postman, N., and C. Weingartner. 1969. *Teaching as a subversive activity*. New York: Delacourte.

Ray M., and M. Myers. 1986. *Creativity in business*. Garden City, NY: Doubleday.

Reich, R. 1992. *The work of nations*. New York: Vintage.

Roberts, A. D., and Cawelti, G. 1984. *Redefining general education in the American high school*. Alexandria, VA: Association of Supervision and Curriculum Development.

Roszak, T. 1994. *The cult of information*. Berkeley: University of California Press.

Rubik, B. 1994. Personal communication.

Russell, P. 1983. *The global brain*. Los Angeles: Tarcher.

Samples, B. 1993. *The metaphoric mind: A celebration of creative consciousness*. Torrance, CA: Jalmar.

Schaer, W. 1988, Winter. Designing for Gaia. *The Quest*.

Schlesinger, A.M., Jr. 1986. *Cycles of American history*. New York: Houghton-Mifflin.

Schmid, C. n.d. Workshop flyer.

Senge, P. 1990. *The fifth discipline*. New York: Doubleday Currency.

Silberman, J. 1970. *Crisis in the classroom*. New York: Random House.

Skolimowski, H. 1984. *The theatre of the mind*. Wheaton, IL: Theosophical Publishing House.

Smith, H. 1995. *Rethinking America*. New York: Random House.

Sternberg, R. 1987, October. *Mind/Brain Bulletin*.

Symington, D., and J. Novak. 1982. Teaching children how to learn. *The Educational Magazine*, 39(5).

Taba, H. 1982. *Curriculum development: Theory and practice*. New York: Harcourt, Brace and World.

Tarnas, R. 1991. *The passion of the Western mind*. New York: Ballantine.

Tart, C. 1987. *Waking up*, Boston: Shambhala.

Tart, C. 1994. Who Might Survive The Death of the Body. Presentation at the Institute of Noetic Science Conference, Chicago.

Toffler, A. 1971. *Future shock*. New York: Bantam.

Van Matre, S. 1972. *Acclimitization*. Martinsville, IN: American Camping Association.

Van Matre, S. 1974. *Acclimatizing sunship earth*. Martinsville, IN: American Camping Association.

Wheatley, M. 1992. *Leadership and the new science*. San Francisco: Berrett-Koehler.

Whitehead, A. N. 1957. *The aims of education*. New York: Free Press.

Wilber, L. 1981. *No boundaries*. Boston: Shambhala.

Wilhelm, K. 1976. *Where late the sweet birds sang*. New York: Harper & Row.

Winter, R. 1994, June 13-19. Rwanda, Up close and horrible. *Washington Post Weekly Edition*.